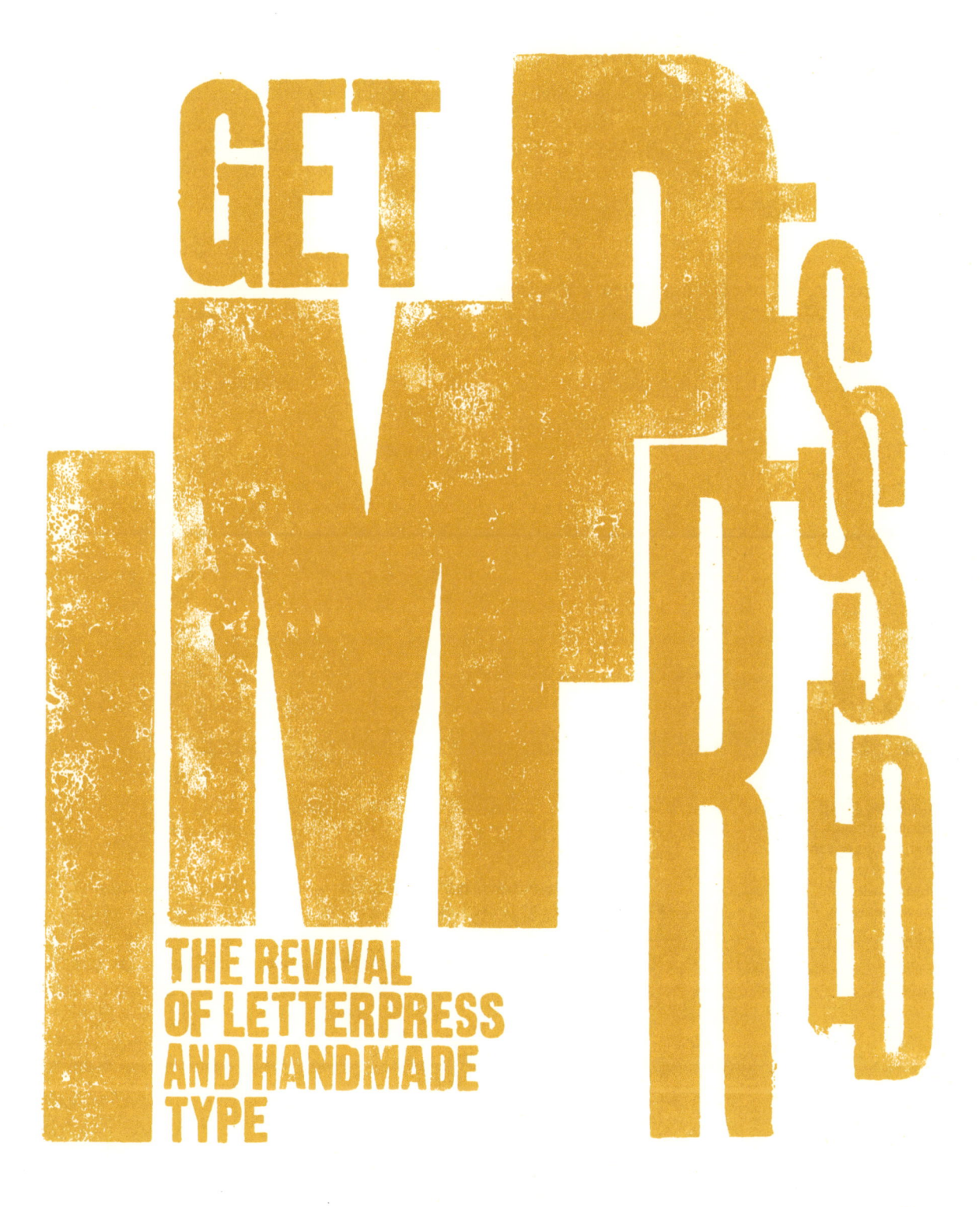

# GET IMPRESSED

## THE REVIVAL OF LETTERPRESS AND HANDMADE TYPE

HOAKI

EDITED BY WANG SHAOQIANG

# HOAKI

C/ Ausiàs March, 128
08013 Barcelona, Spain
T. 0034 935 952 283
F. 0034 932 654 883
info@hoaki.com
www.hoaki.com

hoaki_books

Get Impressed
The Revival of Letterpress and Handmade Type

ISBN: 978-84-17656-37-9

Copyright © 2021 by Sandu Publishing Co., Ltd.
Copyright © 2021 by Hoaki Books, S.L.
for sale in Europe and America

Sponsored by Design 360° — Concept & Design Magazine
Edited, produced, book design, concepts & art direction by
Sandu Publishing Co., Ltd.
info@sandupublishing.com

Chief Editor: Wang Shaoqiang
Executive Editor: Zhang Zhonghui
Copy Editing: Palmiche Press
Designer: Su Zhenhua
Cover Design: Alan Kitching

All rights reserved. The total or partial reproduction of this book, its transmission in any form or by any means or procedure, whether electronic or mechanical, including photocopying, recording or incorporation into an electronic storage and retrieval system, and the distribution of copies of the work through rental or public lending are not permitted without prior authorisation from the publisher.

D.L.: B 9921-2021
Printed in China

# CONTENTS

**Preface** — **006**
By David Wolske

**01** **History of Letterpress and Its Impact on Modern Typography** — **009**

**02** **Process of Letterpress Printing** — **017**

**03** **Letterpress Artists and Printmakers** — **021**

| | | | |
|---|---|---|---|
| Alan Kitching | 022 | Brad Vetter | 060 |
| David Wolske | 032 | Chris Chandler | 070 |
| Tom Boulton | 042 | Bart Heesen | 082 |
| Jessica Spring | 050 | | |

**04** **Letterpress Factories, Initiatives, Museums, etc.** — **095**

| | | | |
|---|---|---|---|
| Clawhammer Press | 096 | Ri Xing Type Foundry | 138 |
| Tipoteca Italiana | 108 | The School of Bad Printing | 146 |
| Gingerly Press | 120 | North or Nowt | 160 |
| p98a | 130 | | |

## 05 More Letterpress Projects... 171

| | |
|---|---|
| Infinitive Factory | 172 |
| If Earth Is Our Mother | |
| —Coffee Grounds Candles | 174 |
| Wedding Pass Set | 176 |
| The 2019 Letterpress Calendar | 178 |
| Chalvin Paris | 180 |
| Muchacha | 181 |
| Happy White Year | 182 |
| Calendar 2018 | 184 |
| Sunshine Is a Friend of Mine | 186 |
| MAKE 100—Letterpress Coasters | 187 |
| Victor Weiss Studio Visual Brand | 188 |
| Maison Emilienne | 190 |
| Pink Holographic | 191 |
| Coinfinity | 192 |
| Maldini Studios | 193 |
| Quer kommuniziert | 194 |
| Proclamation Whiskey | 196 |
| The Work Room by Brychcy | 198 |
| Ben Chen Photography #3 | 199 |
| Letterpress Book | 200 |
| Yu-Chen Business Card | 201 |
| Raw Wine | 202 |
| Sorry Mom Tattoo Studio | 204 |
| MAYK | 206 |
| Anthology of an Object | 207 |
| A6 Notebook | 208 |
| Letterpress Typeset Namecard V18 | 209 |
| Tapui, destilado de pulque | 210 |
| Business Card Design for Veyond | 211 |
| Kinto Cacao | 212 |
| Business Card Design for Black Story | 213 |
| Pockets Full of Change | 214 |
| Karol Kowalski | 216 |
| Restore | 217 |
| Dream Pool of Gutenberg | 218 |
| Fade to Blue | 220 |
| Tarjetas Letterpress | 222 |
| Sole & Diego, Wedding Invitations | 223 |
| Horitaro Tattoo Studio | 224 |
| Xmas and New Year Card 2020–2021 | 225 |
| Music in Print Collection | 226 |
| Keiros Estilistas | 228 |
| OBJM Conservation Studio | 229 |
| A Book of Helium | 230 |
| Prince Dining Room | 232 |

## Index 233

## Acknowledgements 240

# PREFACE

By David Wolske

Letterpress printing is painstakingly slow. It demands patience and rigorous attention to detail. It requires tons of equipment, literally. The presses, metal and wood types, furniture, paper, ink, and other necessary sundries are bulky, difficult to move, and take up a lot of floor space. The final prints are often imperfect, no matter how experienced and skilled the press operator. Despite all this, letterpress printing continues to grow in popularity. So, why is this archaic process still thriving over half a millennium after its invention? What makes letterpress a vital and relevant creative practice?

Letterpress may be old, but it's adaptable. Augmenting this antique process with new technologies expands its already abundant creative possibilities. Early adopters of digital tools have been experimenting with laser cutters, CNC routers, and 3D printers to make movable type and relief printing matrices for decades. Virgin Wood Type, Moore Wood Type, Wood Type Customs, Mark McKellier and Ryan Molloy are just a few businesses and individuals incorporating cutting-edge technology into their workflow. They manufacture revival wood type fonts that make it possible for contemporary printers to use rare nineteenth-century designs. But they also build on traditional techniques and depart from derivative typographic styles to create fresh new fonts for the twenty-first century and beyond. Digital tools also have utility beyond making movable type and modular image blocks for letterpress printing. Enterprising designers like Steve Garst of the Provisional Press and Tom Boulton (a.k.a. Type Tom) are using laser cutters and 3D printers to fabricate kits of parts that assemble into consumer-grade tabletop proofing presses. Because of its enduring appeal and versatility, letterpress links generations and attracts more young creatives every day.

These modern designers find a connection to the roots of their craft through letterpress printing. Points, picas, leading, kerning, ligature, lockup, uppercase, and lowercase—these words, recognisable to most graphic artists through layout and design applications, all descend from the letterpress lexicon. Other familiar terms derived from letterpress include logo (short for logotype), stereotype, cliché, and the phrase "out of sorts." The vast majority of presses and movable metal and wood types used by today's letterpress printers were purchased, salvaged, or inherited from an older printer after decades of stewardship. It's nearly impossible not to wonder how many hands before yours held a composing stick; how many books, brochures, broadsides, greeting cards and wedding announcements did this worn font of 12-point Caslon print? By adapting traditional tools and techniques to complement their current digital workflow, contemporary designers become part of a fraternity of makers that's over 500 years old.

The love of letterpress is not exclusive to graphic designers and visual artists. Letterpress is inherently interdisciplinary. It's taught in libraries, printmaking, design, history, and creative writing courses at universities worldwide. Private studios and non-profit community centres offer seminars and workshops taught by artists and designers who specialise in traditional and experimental approaches to typography, wood engraving, linoleum cutting, photopolymer plates, poetry and more.

Nowhere is the cross-pollination of letterpress and other creative practices more apparent than in artist books. Pioneers like Julie Chen of Flying Fish Press and the members of Shift-lab (Katie Baldwin, Denise Bookwalter, Sarah Bryant, Macy Chadwick, and Tricia Treacy) combine letterpress and numerous analog and digital methods to create beautiful, conceptually-driven 2D and 3D works that defy categorisation.

Making intricate, interdisciplinary work using a mix of old and new equipment means letterpress artists must frequently collaborate with a broadly knowledgeable network. That's why passionate communities of printers all over the world gather online and in-person to preserve stories, legacies, traditions, tools, and techniques. Museums, organisations, and social media platforms offer centralised locations for a wide range of letterpress events and activities.

Since 2008, hundreds of designers, typographers, artists, and craftspeople from across the globe travel to Two Rivers, Wisconsin, every November to attend the Wayzgoose hosted by the Hamilton Wood Type & Printing Museum. Like Hamilton, the Gutenberg-Museum in Mainz, Germany, and Tipoteca Italiana, in Cornuda, Italy welcome international visitors for tours, exhibitions, workshops and artist residencies.

In addition to museums, dozens of organisations cater to enthusiastic letterpress amateurs, professionals and academics. Two venerable examples are the British Printing Society and the Amalgamated Printers' Association. Ladies of Letterpress is a vibrant international trade organisation "dedicated to the proposition that a woman's place is in the print shop." Letterpress Workers (LPW), started in 2012 by Officina Tipografica Novepunti, is a short-term collaborative artist residency for printers from Europe and the Americas. Letterpress Educators of Art and Design (LEAD) is a new organisation founded by Erin Beckloff, Stephanie Carpenter, Allison Fisher, Katherine Fries, Vida Sačić, and myself to advance research and scholarship and substantiate the value of letterpress education. In July 2020, LEAD organised and hosted Makeready 2020, a virtual symposium connecting over 150 letterpress educators from a dozen countries.

While less hands-on, social media platforms offer informative and entertaining views into hundreds of letterpress workshops, studios, basements, and garages. Letterpress United, a Facebook page with over 2,200 followers, is "dedicated to live streams from letterpress printers and artists from all over the world." Even more impressive (pun intended), the Instagram hashtag #letterpress has amassed over 1,000,000 posts where individual printers, museums, and organisations share images of their presses, type collections, and works-in-progress. Likes and follows on social media, membership in organisations, and attendance to printing museums multiply every year, proving that the accessibility, versatility, and unlimited creative power of letterpress is contagious and addicting.

*Get Impressed* showcases many of the artists, designers, crafters, and makers who continue to push the boundaries of a medium whose creative potential is inexhaustible. The people and projects included in this book represent a timely cross-section of a growing revival of letterpress printed art and design. As interest continues to increase, technologies merge, communities grow, and creative boundaries expand, I predict the future of letterpress will look a lot like its past—long and colourful.

# 01

## History of Letterpress and Its Impact on Modern Typography

# Letterpress Art Impresses the World

• **Movable Type Moves History**

There are several hypotheses on the origin of movable type. And neither the place of origin nor the inventor is clearly known.

The Chinese believe that the earliest known printing started during the Sui and Tang dynasties. In this period, Buddhism had widely spread throughout East Asia and this greatly resulted in the flourishing of woodblock printing. Artisans carved out images and text on a piece of wood, then applied ink, and covered it with paper. The ink served to transfer the image and text to the paper. The process had to be repeated several times to make a clear copy. The earliest example was the *Great Spell of Unsullied Pure Light* printed during the Tang dynasty.

The disadvantages of woodblock printing are obvious, not only because of the complexity of engraving and inking but also because the woodblocks are easily damaged. Even a small blemish requires remaking the entire piece.

1. Gutenberg. Image from Wikimedia Commons.

2. Shikei matrix1. Image from Wikimedia Commons.

3. Employee of the printing company, Offizin Haag-Drugulin. Image from Wikimedia Commons.

4. Garamond type ft-ligature. Image from Wikimedia Commons.

| 1. | 2. | 3. | 4. |

In the 11th century CE, Bi Sheng invented movable type with clay. This very early movable type was almost identical to the modern movable type used presently. Artisans produce types, then create the composition and design the layout. They subsequently use fire to affix the types on an iron plate, and as the final process, they perform the inking and printing.

The advantage of movable type printing is that the types can be reused and the compositions are easy to compose. The first movable type was made of clay, but later different materials such as pottery, porcelain, copper, and wood were utilized. Although Chinese artisans made books using movable type during that period, no surviving bound copies, only individual written records, seem to be in existence in China. The oldest surviving book produced with metallic movable type is the *Jikji* (the abbreviated title of a Korean Buddhist document whose title can be translated as *Anthology of Great Buddhist Priests' Zen Teaching*) which was printed in Korea in the 14th century.

Nevertheless, artisans in East Asia invented movable type. Their invention and widespread use predates the work of Johannes Gutenberg, the acknowledged inventor of movable type in Europe, by four centuries. And even *Jikji*, the first-ever metallic movable type book, was printed 78 years before the *Gutenberg Bible*.

There is no evidence that Gutenberg was influenced by the technology from East Asia. It is pointless to argue that Gutenberg was the first person in history to invent and produce movable type, just as it is meaningless for the Chinese and Koreans to debate from where movable type originates. Just as James Watt was regarded as a figure in inventing the steam engine, letterpress was hardly invented by any one artisan alone. The process of inventing a great new instrument rarely occurs in isolation. It is more like a gradual iteration, the accumulation and development through knowledge, skills, persistence and wisdom. The cultural influence of letterpress has had a more profound impact on human civilisation because so many people were instrumental in its development than if the letterpress had been invented and developed by one person.

As a result of the invention of movable type, culture and information have been more accessible to the civil class; the privileged classes and aristocrats of the past were no longer solely triumphant on their access to knowledge. Commerce also received a boost during this period.

The earliest brand advertisement in China can be traced back to the 12th century. The piece of "White Rabbit" copper plate for letterpress is an advertisement of a needle brand that was designed and used in 1127. This advertisement, which seems to have a sense of modern design, may have been popular at that time.

Book publishing and printing also entered a period of prosperity. Buddhist scriptures, Chinese classic texts, literature, novels, and a collection of poems were largely printed, spreading culture to the urban civil class. Even the political forum, which used to be dominated by royal families and the privileged classes, had started to be replaced by the competent officers raised from various classes, most of whom came from the regions with thriving publishing and printing industries. The imperial examination system, which started during the Tang Dynasty and lasted 400 years, had a profound influence on China, both on social and political levels.

In Europe, the *Gutenberg Bible*, produced by Johannes Gutenberg, is regarded by many people as the first great sign of Renaissance and Reformation.

5. This is typesetting equipment on display at Beamish Museum. Image from Wikimedia Commons.

6-7. *Gutenberg Bible*. Images from Wikimedia Commons.

The privileged class and the absolute truth established during medieval times, which were propagated through manuscripts and religious Christian dogma, were challenged by this new technology. Back then, printing was the only tool for humans to seek their own paths towards knowledge and truth other than the fatalism of the Middle Ages.

Within the next four centuries, Europe witnessed the Renaissance, the Reformation, the Age of Enlightenment, and other events that forever changed the history of humankind. Europeans revived and promoted the Greek ideal of "man is the measure of all things", which influenced not only the construction of social theories but also artistic movements such as the Bauhaus.

At the same time, the printing press greatly impacted the concepts of nation-states and imagined communities. The spread of print capitalism was instrumental for human beings to build their world views, through education, and to instill a common idea and national destiny into their minds since those early years.

Lithography was invented in the 18th century, and was followed by offset printing and hot metal typesetting in the 19th century. These technologies improved the efficiency in the production of newspapers and stamps. In the mid-20th century, the invention of digital typesetting allowed us to completely overcome the fragility of plates and movable types, and massively improved the productivity of printing again.

The printing revolution, which began in the 15th century and lasted for almost five centuries, has completely changed the definition of art and the path of its dissemination.

Works of art, the only creations that had ever been made with originality and ingenuity, became "The Work of Art in the Age of Mechanical Reproduction" (the term by Walter Benjamin). And the beauty of this ancient craft profoundly vanished when the physical and cultural locale and authenticity were broken.

John Berger claimed that in the age of mechanical reproduction, a piece of art can be torn into pieces, and we can only see the artist's real intention in museums. The majority of audiences appreciate art in a relatively fixed size in books or on screens—zoomed in or zoomed out disproportionately without understanding the original meanings the artist wanted to convey.

## • The Work of Art in the Age of Mechanical Reproduction

Let us admit it. It was the birth of mechanical reproduction that made designers become pioneers. Many of them, if born 500 years earlier, would simply be called "craftsmen".

Before Gutenberg, those who created illuminated manuscripts were artists, but they were illustrators and calligraphers as well. After Gutenberg, due to the necessity of mass media, the fields of font design and typography were slowly developed. These fields were specialised and standardised to norms.

Before the 18th century, independent printers like Nicolas Jenson and Aldus Manutius and their history of struggles were well known. But beginning in the 18th century, the era of mass communication of art and of type design began with the emergence of William Caslon, John Baskerville, Firmin Didot, Giambattista Bodoni, Edward Johnston and Eric Gill.

Although the age of mechanical reproduction had a set of strict technical requirements, the talents' inspiration and personal style were not buried. They used their creations to announce the attitude that art should convey: adapting to and using the medium; creating a personal style; reproducing and spreading on a

8. Numbering for letterpress. Image from Wikimedia Commons.

large scale. Their artworks were more often found in newspapers, advertisements, branding materials, flyers, books, and even public spaces. Most of them may not have achieved the same level of fame as Leonardo da Vinci, Michelangelo, and other artists, but it doesn't mean their work wouldn't spread widely. For example, the mural of the Sistine Chapel is magnificent, but does it really influence more people than the Eric Gill typefaces on the titles published by Penguin Books?

The more personalized works appeared in the Art Deco movement, Russian Constructivism, Bauhaus, Hochschule für Gestaltung, Ulm, and Swiss Style. They represented the birth of modern design. Cassandre, El Lissitzky, Moholy-Nagy, Max Bill, Herbert Bayer, Adrian Frutiger, Armin Hofmann… these are the most famous names of that time. A large number of their masterpieces were letterpress printing works.

However, after the 1960s, letterpress began to be marginalised. Chandler & Price, the most famous and largest print shop at that time, stopped producing machines in 1964. Linotype and Monotype, two of the most prestigious and largest letterpress printers, also stopped producing a wide range of letterpress at the same time and switched to the development of digital typefaces.

As we move to the 21st century, a new renaissance in letterpress printing begins. Of course, people won't return to using letterpress to create abundant communication products. The interesting thing is that more small studios use letterpress printing on a limited scale to create and reproduce objects, such as personal business cards, wedding invitations and posters.

Today, famous artists like Alan Kitching, Erik Spiekermann, Anthony Burrill and Jesus Morentin all run their own type foundries.

## • Type Designer Design Types

In our age, it seems that letterpress has more or less returned to Benjamin's definition of classical art: "Its presence in time and space, its unique existence at the place where it happens to be. This unique existence of the work of art determined the history to which it was subject throughout the time of its existence."

We would certainly question whether such art is comparable to the art that existed before the time of mechanical reproduction.

Let's try to answer this question with Ernst Gombrich's saying: "There really is no such thing as Art. There are only artists." He is not trying to debase the value of art. He just wants to explain that we don't have to sublimate and dogmatise "art" and ignore that artists are actually creators.

Those who use letterpress for creative practice in modern times are certainly artists, but their purpose has long gone beyond what the art forms of the past demanded— serve for worship. Do not forget that the existence of art is determined by history.

Letterpress artist Richard Ardagh defended the value of letterpress printing in an exhibition in 2020. "Letterpress printing is how information was disseminated for over 500 years," according to Ardagh. "We live in a time now where social media gives everyone a platform to express an opinion quickly, but as soon as it's there, it's gone. The permanence and tactility of a beautifully printed poster have much more impact."

Not only Richard, but any artist who works with letterpress, including Alan and Erik, would sum up the appeal of this work as follows: handmade, slow, tactile, real, unchangeable and uncontrollable.

These attributes seem to be universally acknowledged as virtues of letterpress. But from another point of view, these are the disadvantages that have caused letterpress to become a less utilised industrial process as there are faster and newer technologies to spread information more quickly.

Perhaps we have to admit that history spiraled forward. Letterpress is currently experiencing its own time of "Renaissance". Perhaps the biggest reason is simply that artists are tired of the quick and large allocation of information that social media and capitalism deliver.

Gombrich's definition of "artist" should include a rebellion against fashion and paradigm. No artist is satisfied with following others' styles. What artists are passionate about is creating their own styles.

So, why are there so many artists (in this book or not) enthusiastic to create letterpress art? Because they are not just artists who create types. They are artists who create their own types.

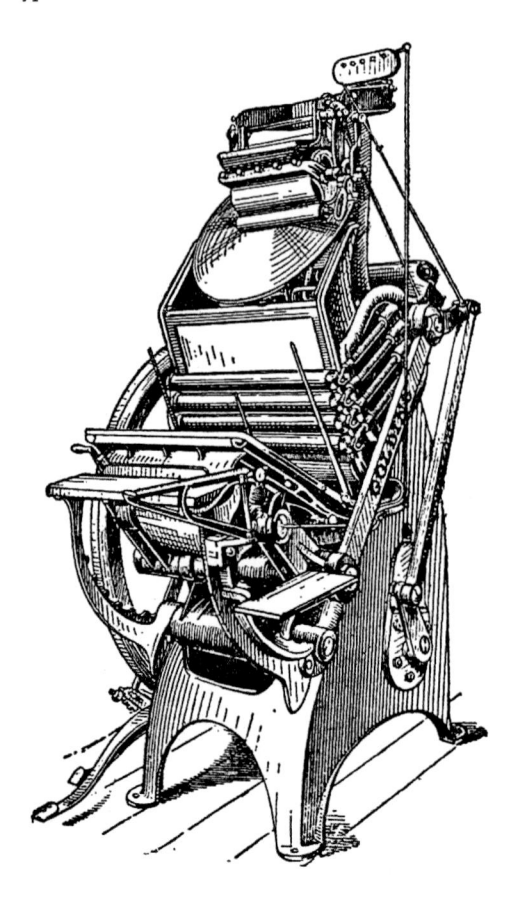

9. The Golding Jobber platen machine, a small but useful platen machine heavily employed in printing houses that specialise in commercial work. Image from Wikimedia Commons.

# 02

# Process of
# Letterpress Printing

# Get Impressed: The Process of Letterpress Printing

The process of letterpress printing consists of four main stages: lettering and illuminating, composition, lock-up and printing.

## Lettering & Illuminating

The first step of letterpress is lettering and illuminating. In the past, artisans would write the characters or design the patterns on a piece of paper, then stick it on the bottom side of a woodblock and engrave it. Later, the process evolved into using a mold shape to cast types. Now, it is much easier to cast type with mechanical production and a laser cutter.

Each Chinese character has a specific type. Due to the large amount of Chinese characters, each foundry produces fonts based on specific needs. Each font consists of 20,000–30,000 characters. The commonly used characters often have backups, so it is difficult to estimate the scale.

Western typography seems to be much simpler as there are fewer than 50 letters. However, counting different glyphs, letter case, and didactic symbols, it is not that easy to design and produce types. Moreover, western typographers not only design and cast types, they also need to produce the illuminated patterns that decorate the text altogether. This is a tradition inherited from the illuminated scripts produced during the middle ages.

The Chinese store types in shelves with plenty of rows. To remember such a large number of types is very difficult. Chinese typographers solve this issue by categorising the types with some principles by writing a poem to make them easier to remember. Europeans, on the other hand, reserve types in a box with uppercase for majuscule and lowercase for minuscule.

Of course, these are general methods in traditional foundries. The artists who often require specific sizes for their creations might have their own way to preserve types.

Process of Letterpress Printing

# Composition

Selecting types and assembling to form the layout is the stage before printing. The person responsible for this stage is a compositor or typesetter.

They pick out the types and illuminations, tie up each line, design the layout and check for errors. During this process, they will use small pieces of bamboo, wood, or lead to ensure each line is straight and to help lock the plate so that the types do not fall off.

Another step is to examine and uniform the heights of types with a block of wood or lead. Otherwise, the result is vague with uneven shades.

In the process of assembling the plates, the artisans invented various methods to overcome problems, and these solutions have been inherited into modern typography and font design. For example, the size of the typeface is measured in points; kerning describes the adjustment of word spacing; leading is used to set the line spacing; the size of the lead block is called *em*, and so on and so forth.

# Lock-up

The carrier for printing was a slate slab in the early days and later it switched to a precisely machined iron casting. Subsequently, strips of different sizes would be inserted to affix the composition. Finally the process of lock-up is performed with screws like quoins and keys.

The strips have various dimensions especially designed for different occasions, ranging from shortest to largest: lead, reglet, quotation to furniture.

1. Photo by Hannes Wolf.

# Printing

The last stage is printing. Artisans would select suitable paper and produce inks before operating the printer.

The paper used for letterpress is soft, spongy, and absorbent, which smoothly leaves marks without excessively distorting the paper. Even worn type can achieve a decent impression.

Once the paper is selected, the artisans would proceed to produce inks. Then they would transfer the inks to the disc and rollers to start the final operation. They would arrange the paper, check the first printed sheet, proofread, and if there were no errors, they would commence the formal printing. After twenty or so impressions, the machine would require to recharge the inks. This process would take place several times by the time the artisans finalized the printing.

Professional heavy machines usually have a set of rollers for colour mixing and printing, while smaller machines usually have only two rollers. But small machines allow the artist to have more space and leeway to experiment with the operation of the press and to produce more creative artwork.

2. Photo by Hello I'm Nik.

# 03

**Letterpress Artists
And Printmakers**

ABOVE US ONLY SKY

John Lennon

"The colour is there to reinforce the logic and the spirit of the subject. The combination of the letterforms and the layout, the colour all combined to express the full meaning of the text."

# ALAN KITCHING

**London, UK**

Born in 1940, Alan Kitching had acquired a love of printing, drawing, and painting whilst at school. By the mid-1950s, he was an apprentice compositor. It was there that he first encountered modern design through magazines such as *Printing Review* and *British Printer*, and became aware of figures such as Jan Tschichold, who influenced his early experiments.

From 1962–1964, he was a technician in hand and line type composition, Department of Printing, at Watford College of Technology. After meeting Anthony Froshaug (the new Senior Lecturer in the School of Art), Alan co-established with Froshaug the experimental printing workshop at Watford College of Technology. He later continued to collaborate with Froshaug on student projects at the Central School of Art and Design, in London.

"I didn't want to be a jobbing printer but I wanted to start out on my own. It was a very precarious thing to do because we were a successful, well-established, graphic design studio and it seemed I was taking a backwards step; it was a bit of a leap in the dark." In 1973, Alan began his own design practice in London. In 1977, he partnered with Derek Birdsall and Martin Lee at Omnific design studio and started letterpress printing there in 1985. He then went on to establish The Typography Workshop in Clerkenwell in 1989. In 1994, Alan was appointed Royal Designer for Industry (RDI) and elected member of Alliance Graphique International (AGI). In addition to teaching there, he is an Honorary Fellow of the Royal College of Art (RCA) and a visiting professor at the University of Arts, London.

1. Alan Kitching is inking movable type.
2. Alan's studio.

Alan is a practitioner of letterpress typographic design and printmaking. He exhibits and lectures across the globe, and is known for his expressive use of wood and metal letterforms in commissions and limited-edition prints. He has a passion for letterpress print using old-style wood and metal blocks in a fine art capacity. He usually starts from the logic which implies the brief and what the subject is about. His work employs vivid colours and characters, blends in his knowledge and experience to tighten the discipline amidst the constraints of typesetting, inking, and repeating as an art form. "I always try to have some logic to the job, to the work. That is really what I find interesting," says Alan.

Alan's work appears in private collections and galleries, and is also featured on everything from magazine and book covers, postage stamps, and theatre posters, to wine labels, billboards, and signage. He continues to influence and inspire a new generation of graphic designers and letterpress enthusiasts across the world.

Get Impressed

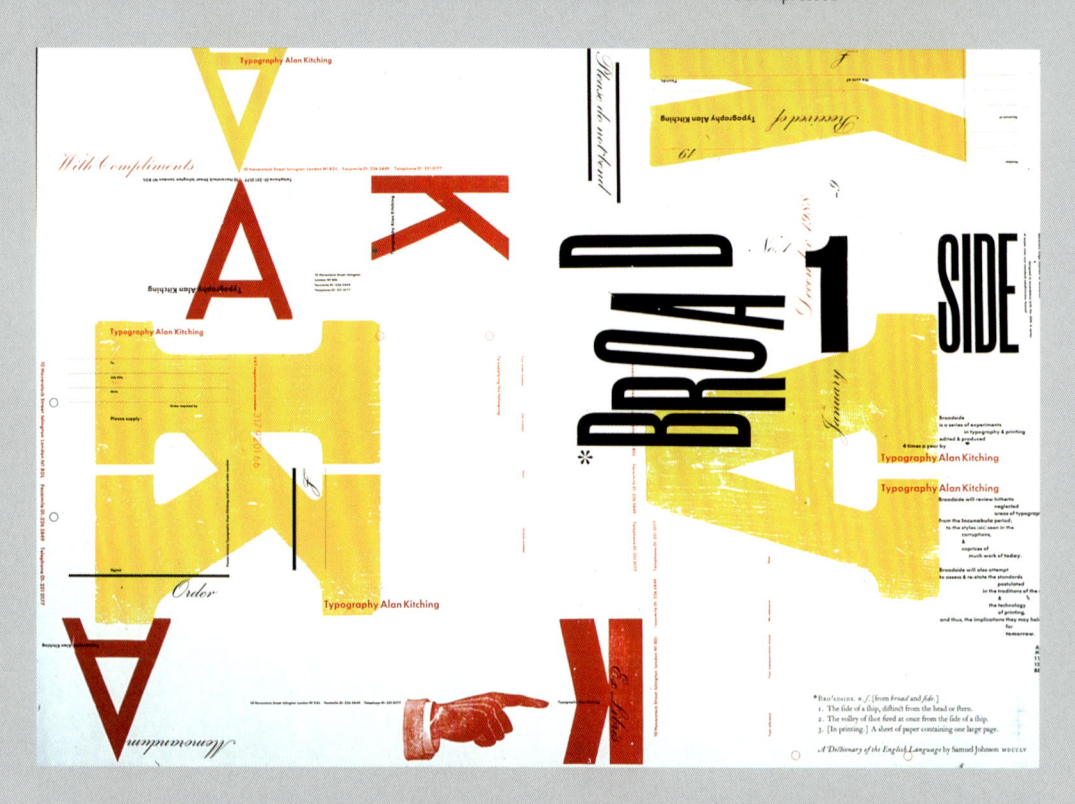

▲ Broadside 1 (1988)
▼ BA 2017/18 (Commission by British Airways for "BA100 - The Art of Travel")
► Parsnip (2001)

Alan Kitching is renowned for his expressive use of wood and metal letterforms in creating visuals for commissions and limited edition prints.

Alan Kitching, the maestro of the letterpress, has spent most of his professional life in exploring and enjoying the iconic landmarks of the city of London as well as its more obscure nooks and crannies.

▲ London Marathon (2012)

▼ Musical Types (2009)

▲ Agincourt (2016)

▼ Fitzrovia (2019, commission by FORA)

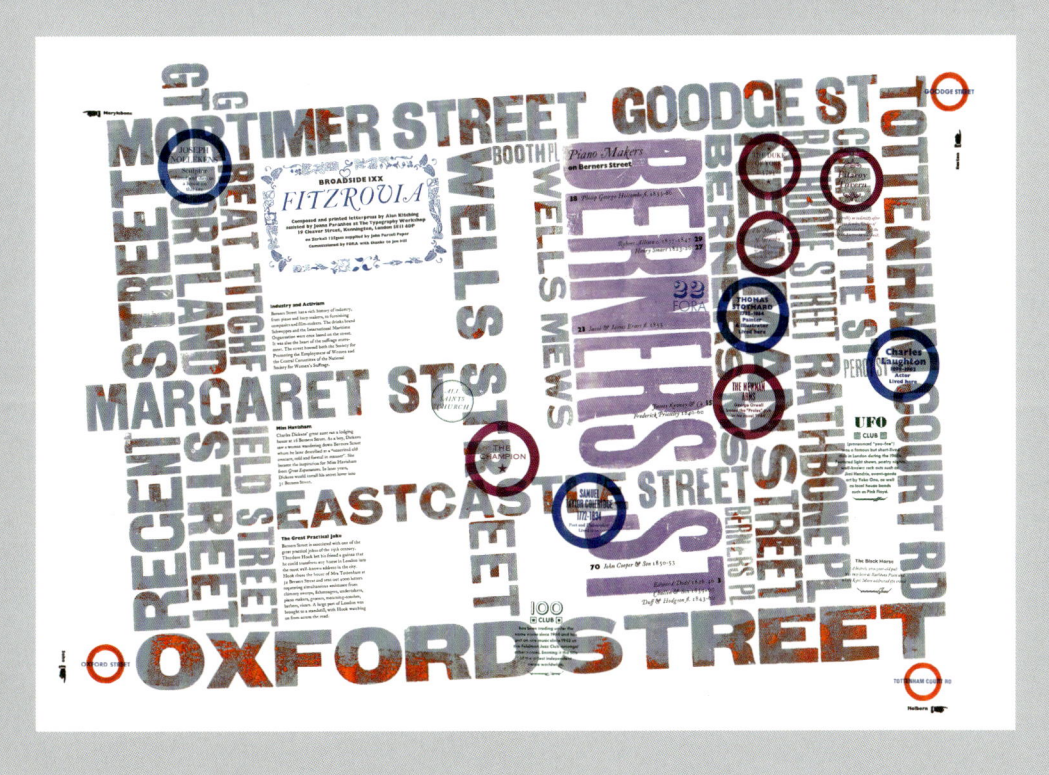

**01  Could you share with us your working process?**

I experiment with the type that is regularly used—inking up and doing a very rough proof of the letters and words. I print on glassine paper which is transparent paper. I make a paper collage, which is a very rough interpretation of the result. Once that collage is done, I then proceed to do a more substantial layout on the press with the finalized blocks. That's how I start.

**02  Your works are described as some bold and colourful spectacle. What's your colour scheme or design philosophy?**

The choice of colour then comes into action because while I'm working out what the subject is about, I'm considering colour and possibilities. Because it's a printed image, I've always tried to get away from the idea that it is a printed image. Because the origin of the printed images was always black and white—the ink was black and the paper was white. And I started to change that concept. About 25 or 30 years ago, I've experimented with colours ever since, but the colour is there to reinforce the logic and the spirit of the subject. So the combination of the letterforms and the layout, the colour all combined to express the full meaning of the text.

**03** *You've said that you're not interested in letterpress printing. How do you keep motivated in an uninterested field?*

That's true in a sense. When I was teaching at the Royal College of Art, I was teaching typography through letterpress. The first thing I said to the students was "I am not interested in letterpress printing", meaning I'm not interested in the technicalities of it, like how the press works with all that technical stuff I was never interested in much. What I'm interested in is the image you get from it.

**04** *Where do you see letterpress printing evolve?*

It's been evolved. It died out in the 70s. I brought it back in the 80s. It's been kind of growing importance in the graphic world ever since. You're quite right. It was interesting. People are using it in photography and filming now. You can do it so much better with a digital camera and even on an iPhone. It's something attractive about the hands-on effect of ink, paper and blocks of wood. It's a very basic thing which has been existing for thousands of years starting from China in woodblock cut. I think people have always been interested in it because it's surrounded by modern technology.

# INTERVIEW WITH

# ALAN KITCHING

# BACK TO THE FUTURE

**Long-Distance Letterpress:**

with **DAVID WOLSKE**

"I honor the history of letterpress by learning from the craftspeople who developed the tools and techniques that make it possible for me to carry their legacies into the future. And I teach new generations what I learn."

# DAVID WOLSKE

**Denton, Texas, USA**

David Wolske is a typographer, graphic designer, artist, and educator. He uses a combination of contemporary and historical processes to transfigure letters, numbers, and punctuation into visual poetry. His abstractions use colour and negative space to communicate the more emotional aspects of written language while inviting the viewers to create their own interpretations.

David's interdisciplinary practice combines digital design tools with the traditions of letterpress and fine art printmaking. He has two distinct modes of working. At times, he works under clear formal rules executed using controlled methods, translating his digital compositions into print on a Vandercook cylinder proofing press with his collection of antique wood and metal types. The predictable nature of this approach gives the artist and his work a sense of mastery. However, he will also improvise at the press with no preconceived notions. This strategy is rooted in curiosity and wonder. Its unpredictable nature leads to learning and discovery and continuously drives his practice forward.

Blending new and old technologies is ultimately about working with the building blocks of language, which themselves are an ancient, continuously evolving technology. David invented a printing technique and named it "isotype printing", a portmanteau of the words "isolate" and "type". By using formal elements of type, like stems, bowls, and serifs, he recasts text into a new kind of tool for communication. The resulting prints offer conceptual dichotomies such as control/chaos, symmetry/asymmetry, and harmony/dissonance.

By deconstructing language to express a more visceral form of communication, David's work playfully subverts the relationship between the hand and the machine.

1. David Wolske's portrait. Photograph by Duston Todd.

2-3. During the working process.

Viewers are often surprised when they learn or realise that the deceptively simple shapes they see in these enigmatic compositions are remixed letters and numbers. By abstracting the alphabet, David transforms the ordinary, or even banal, into something new and unexpected. Talking about the communication between letterpress printing and the viewers, he says, "I hope to communicate intellectually and emotionally. I don't aim to control people's feelings or thoughts. I leave room for them to contribute their own perspective and curiosity, and to decide for themselves what it looks like, what it reminds them of, and how it makes them feel."

Letterpress is traditional media. David elevates it with contemporary design and creative thinking. "Painting, ceramics, sculpture, textiles, printmaking, etc… are all 'traditional'. The media is just a vehicle for creative expression. I honor the history of letterpress by learning from the craftspeople who developed the tools and techniques that make it possible for me to carry their legacies into the future. And I teach new generations what I learn."

David's work is exhibited and collected nationally and internationally. He is a 2020 Leah Hoffmitz Milken Educator Fellow at the Hoffmitz Milken Center for Typography at ArtCenter College of Design, the College Book Art Association 2018 Emerging Educator, 2016 Visiting Artist at Hatch Show Print, and a 2014 Utah Visual Arts Fellow. He is currently an Assistant Professor in the College of Visual Arts & Design at the University of North Texas.

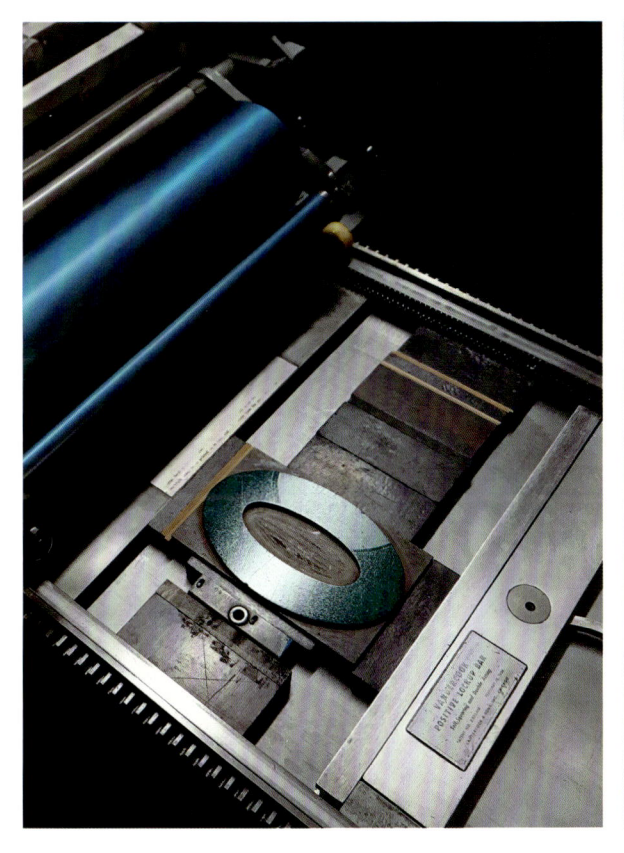

The *Paraphrasing* series investigates the use of negative space as a dynamic compositional component. The abstract imagery combines metal type and rules with wood type that has been masked using David Wolske's unique "isotype" printing method.

Letterpress Artists and Printmakers

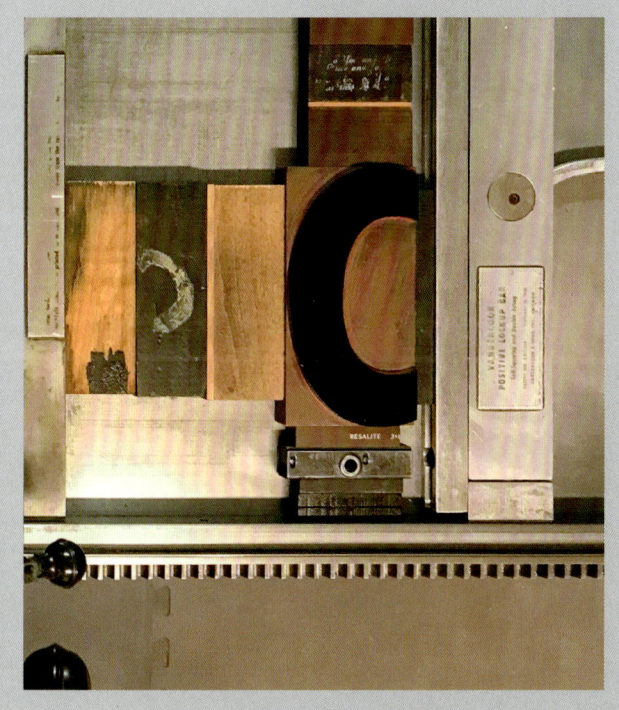

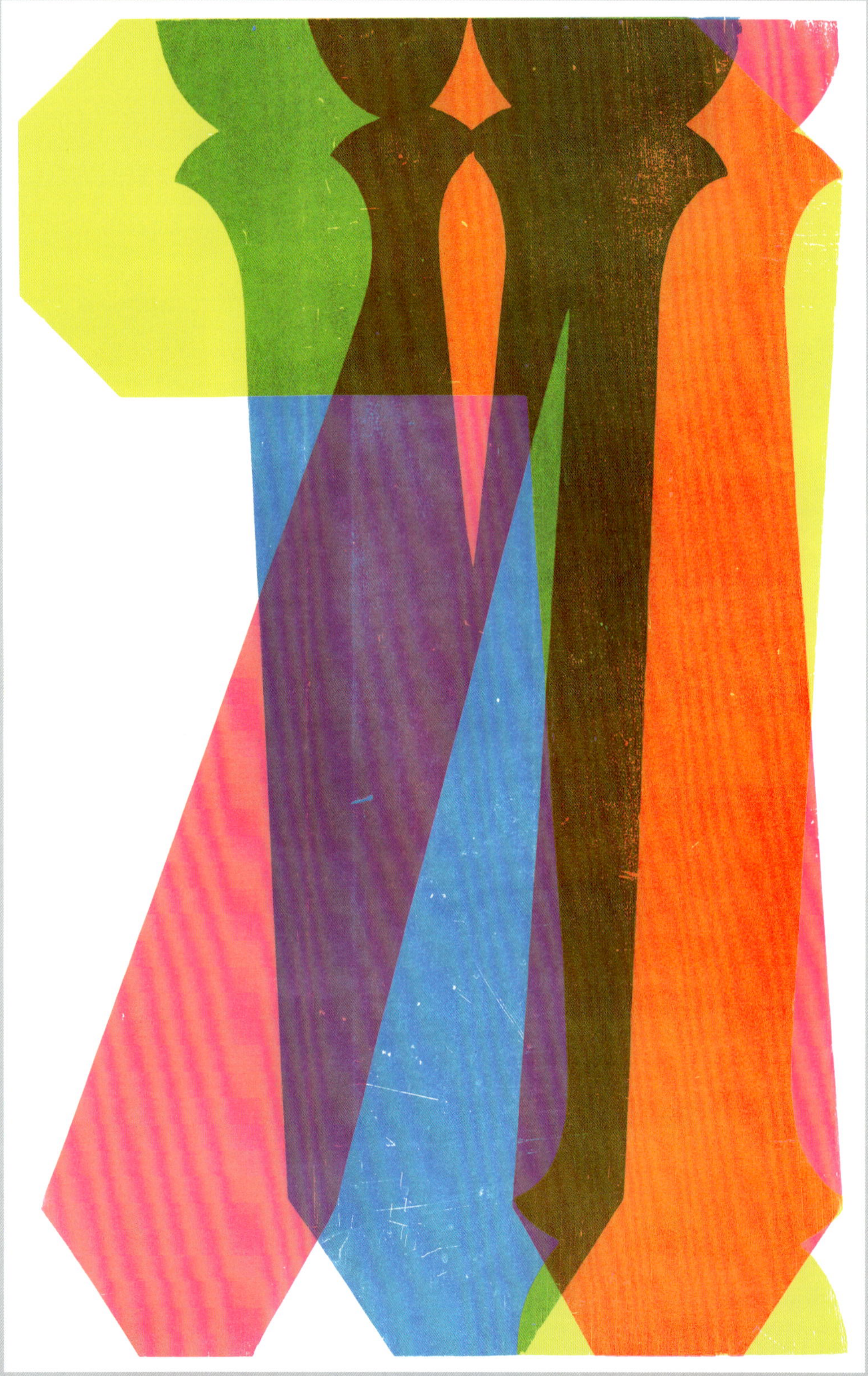

Letterpress Artists and Printmakers

The *Synæsthetica* series—by using larger than life letterforms and arranging the layers to create dynamic colour and shape interactions, David Wolske engages viewers in a vivid trans-sensory dialog. The prints may be experienced individually, but the suite was conceived as an almost infinitely reconfigurable installation. When combined, the prints become a mural which simultaneously alludes to contemporary street art as well as the palimpsest resulting from the paste-over and removal of printed posters, billboards and road signs. Exhibition curators are enlisted as collaborators and encouraged to make creative decisions about orientation and sequence.

# INTERVIEW WITH DAVID WOLSKE

*01 The clean lines and simple shapes of your letters and words belie a complex approach to image-making. Could you share with us your working process?*

My process always begins with a conceptual question or technical challenge. Two questions that have been driving my recent work are: "What might the future of letterpress printing with wood type look like?" "What new typographic forms exist within a collection of antique wood type fonts?"

Once I decide on a motivating challenge or concept, I go through the stages of the design process. I research by looking through my collection of wood type, searching for a range of letterforms that offer variety in their stroke construction—vertical, horizontal, diagonal, curved. If I don't already have a proof of the selected blocks, I use one of my presses and black ink to pull a high-quality print. I scan the prints at high resolution and add them to my digital library. Using the scans from my library, I design prototypes using Adobe Photoshop. I can experiment faster and more freely this way. When I discover a digital composition that I resonate with, I refine it until I'm satisfied with the design. To ensure perfect registration, I print out colour separations on my black and white laser printer and create a 100%-scale paste-up.

*02 Why do you choose to work in this experimental and abstract style?*

My style has evolved in response to all of my influences and through a desire to discover new possibilities for the letterpress medium. I've always been drawn to abstract, experimental and conceptual art. Some of my earliest influences include Alexander Calder, Louise Nevelson, Robert Rauschenberg, Franz Kline, Jackson Pollock, Mark Rothko, Ellsworth Kelly and Sol Lewitt.

When I first started letterpress printing, I studied the techniques and traditions of the craft and trade. As I gained confidence in my technical abilities, I pushed myself to experiment more. Though I have profound respect for the amazingly skilled printers of the past, I'm not interested in reproducing what they've already perfected. I found inspiration in the work of designers and artists who pushed the boundaries of letterpress, people like H.N. Werkman, Piet Zwart, Wolfgang Weingart, Alan Kitching, Karel Martens and Jim Sherraden.

**03  Improvisation is important to your creating. Why? How do you visualise an idea to graphic design?**

Improvisational design helps me stay present in the creative process. Making spontaneous decisions means I'm responding to the relationships of content, form and counter form, colour and texture. My improvised compositions develop organically and intuitively, but I'm simultaneously honing my ability to rationalise my design choices. The position, scale, orientation, and opacity of every element is a conscious choice that's relative to what I'm seeing and feeling in the moment.

**04  You strive to push letterpress forward and explore its possibilities. What possibilities do you think letterpress contains? And where do you see letterpress evolving?**

The possibilities of letterpress are infinite. I primarily work with the Latin alphabet, which has 26 letters, plus punctuation and 10 Arabic numerals. Multiply the letters, punctuation, and numerals by the many thousands of typefaces manufactured in many dozens of sizes. The number of variations is literally limitless. Every day, letterpress moves further away from its commercial origins as a means of reproduction and dissemination. As artists combine new technologies with traditional tools, we're going to see more experimentation. I see letterpress evolving into an ever more dynamic creative practice and a recognised printmaking discipline.

# THE WILL TO DO WILL SEE US THROUGH

"We all have to look to the future and work out how we can take things forward. Traditions, the modern world and the future can fuse and work together and help each other grow and develop for future generations."

# TOM BOULTON

**Sussex, UK**

Born in Arundel, West Sussex, Tom Boulton studied Typographic Design at the London College of Printing basing himself in London for his founding years before relocating to live and work by the sea and grow his type and printing press collection. His love for printing started in childhood. He loves being creative. "No two days are ever really the same and that's the way I like it. One day I may be doing maintenance, the next designing, printing or making. I like to feel free creatively, being in a workshop filled with type, presses, ink and tools gives me that sense of freedom."

Tom is a typographic designer and letterpress printer who started buying letterpress machines and type about ten years ago. Language and the way words flow are an important part of Tom's work. They are the starting point for all his design and print projects. His natural calling is to learn new skills, often skills that are considered obsolete or dead to bring them back, revive interest and then use them in a contemporary context. This blends perfectly with his obsession with hand printing, hand-making and collecting old machinery.

Tom has collected lots of old stuff. "I'm an avid collector so wherever I go I am always on the lookout for some type or a press or anything interesting. I buy stuff at book fairs, online and sometimes I get offered presses or type from people who were in the trade and want to make sure it goes to someone who will love it and will use it. So basically anywhere and everywhere." The Sussex workshop now houses around 13 presses and a large selection of both wood and lead type. The workshop is a space to inspire contemporary typographic creativity and embrace the true craft of letterpress.

1. Tom at the Skoll World Forum 2019. Photo by Oxford Atelier.

2-3. Tom's wood type collection. Photos by Rob Luckins.

044

Tom has also given out workshops to the public. He aimed to get as many people as possible to interact with printing. It's something that has become a regular part of his life. "It's really interesting to watch people interact with the presses and type. Letterpress is like no other process, the restrictive nature is something I really enjoy going through when I run workshops as different personalities deal with this differently. Some fight it and try and force things to work and others accept and embrace it, both are great to work with. I think it is really important to understand and pass on traditions; letterpress has such a rich and great history of design and so much to offer contemporary designers," says Tom.

With over ten years of experience in letterpress printing and designing for both trade and personal clients, Tom has worked with a wide variety of people and organisations on contemporary design and print commissions for clients including Tate Modern, Southbank Centre, V&A, Fortnum & Mason, and the Design Museum. He uses all of his experience on commissions being a typographic artist, product developer, hand manufacture, educator, and teacher of letterpress, and event or experience organiser. For those who want to pursue letterpress, Tom says, "Play, experiment, enjoy, take your time to develop and try not to think too much. There is far too much emphasis on being productive and not enough on developing and just doing something because you enjoy it."

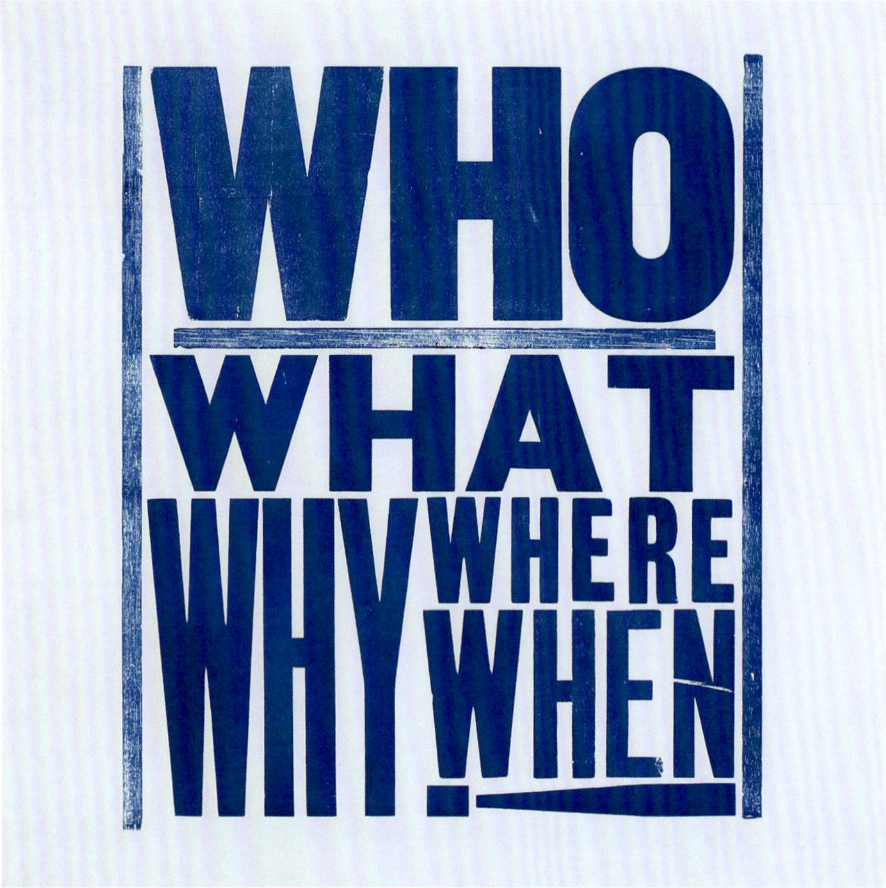
WHO
WHAT
WHY WHERE
WHEN

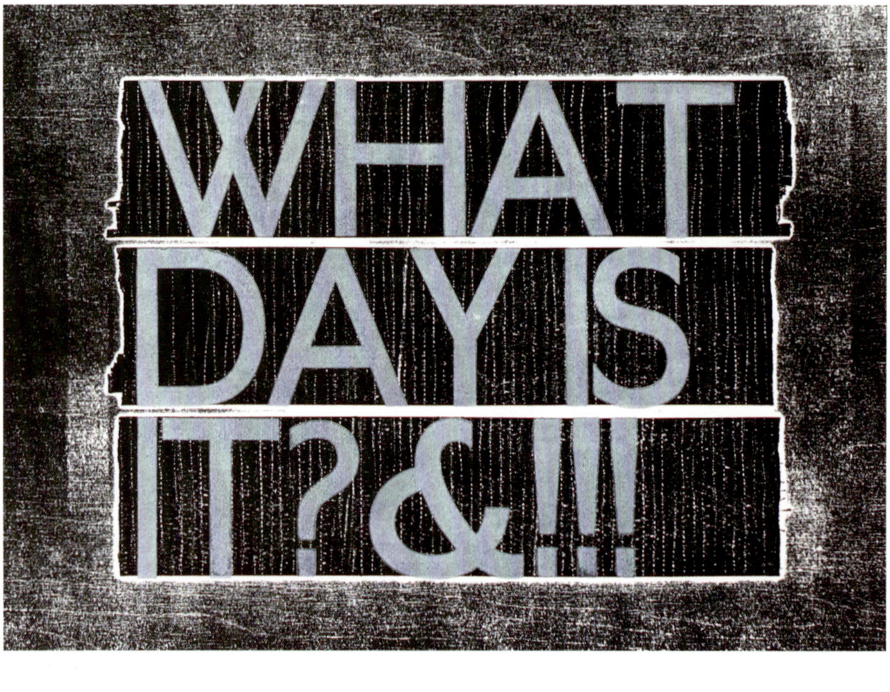
WHAT
DAY IS
IT?&!!!

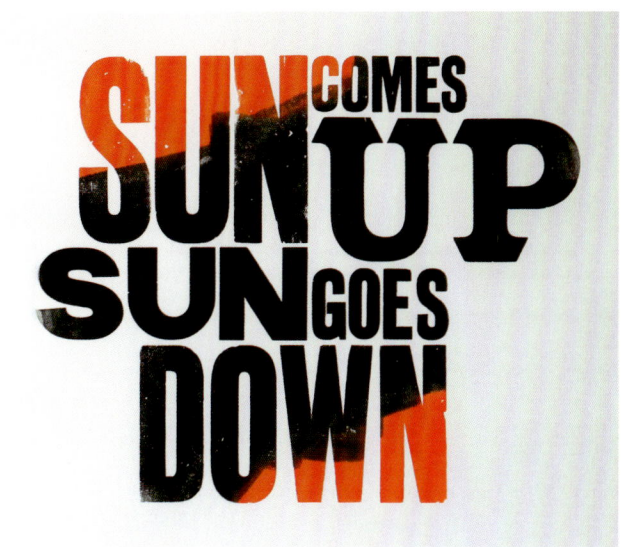

◀▲ During the Covid-19 lockdown, Tom created a series of self-initiated prints including: Who What Why Where When, What Day Is It, Today's The Day, Sun Comes Up Sun Goes Down. Photos by Tom Boulton.

▼ Tom's F-Press and handmade product, Press On card.

# INTERVIEW WITH

# TOM BOULTON

***01 What's your usual process of designing and making? How do you visualize an idea into letterpress printing?***

I am always driven towards phrases and word combinations that sound nice or roll a certain way—I like the way words feel; I usually start with how words feel rather than how they look. Letterpress is like no other process, you are incredibly restricted in the basic sense you have a set amount of fonts and they are the size they are! Meaning you can go into printing a new design and have the idea in your head and the process forces you to adapt the design so you create something completely different. Often the things I print that I like the most are the ones where the type almost composed itself; I really enjoy this organic part of the process.

***02 F-Press is your new project which combines new ways of manufacturing. How did you come up with this idea?***

I work a lot on private projects that I often don't really tell people about. It is nice to just do stuff for myself sometimes. The F-Press has been one of these projects and has been a long time coming. For years I have thought about having a smaller lightweight press that I could take out and about easily. Then Covid-19 happened. I had to close my workshop doors and shield and like a lot of us, I thought long and hard about: What is the future? I set up a small workshop in my garage at home and started working with a 3D printer and a small modified CNC machine. I just started playing around really to see what was possible; I designed parts, made them, and then just tested them out to see what I liked and what worked. I started sharing images of the F-Press developments on my social media and I got a lot of really positive feedback. The idea grew and the design developed into what it is now. I wanted to make a modern interpretation of a letterpress printing press, one that is not unlike traditional presses, a press that can be a real introduction to letterpress. The ultimate aim is to get people printing whether that is at home or in education settings. I decided as 2020 was such an unpredictable year to roll the dice a bit and run a crowdfunder for the project to see if people really are interested in this sort of development. To my amazement they were, and the project funded at 349%.

**03  You have been making new wood types for a long time. Traditional letterpress printing has been facing challenges in this digital era. What do you think of this phenomenon?**

I have been playing around with type-making for around a year. It came out of the basic question: How do I get more wood type? Obviously, the answer is to make your own! The increase in interest in letterpress has led to an increase in prices for equipment and particularly type! I have been really fascinated and somewhat obsessed for a long time about designing my own fonts and then making my own wood type. Letterpress in the modern era can still be what it has always been, the act of composing moveable type and printing it with ink and pressure. We all have to look to the future and work out how we can take things forward. Traditions, the modern world, and the future can fuse and work together and help each other grow and develop for future generations.

**04  In your opinion, what is the future of letterpress?**

The future is so hard to predict right now! I have worked with letterpress for around 15 years and I have seen its popularity and interest grow a lot. Interestingly this popularity and interest have grown at the same time as social media, a time where we can all look beyond our own four walls and delve into each other's worlds and lives. As we look to grow and develop, we look more at what each other does and I see the future as a bright place filled with opportunities. And no matter what happens, you can guarantee that people like me will be in their workshops somewhere in the world playing with some type and printing something nice.

SPRING

TIDINGS!

"My craft continues to focus on amplifying voices needing to be heard, telling stories in a new way, and ultimately, preservation through production."

# JESSICA SPRING

**Tacoma, Washington, USA**

Proprietor Jessica Spring started setting cold type on a Compugraphic EditWriter 7300 phototypesetting machine (a huge console with a big green screen) in 1982 as an undergraduate English major, beginning a lifelong interest in typography. She learned to set real metal type in 1989 and has been a letterpress printer ever since, even inventing Daredevil Furniture for the composition of metal type in circles, curves and angles. "Working as a partner in a small graphic design firm in the late 1980s, we incorporated letterpress printing in our services, along with educating clients on this 'new' process and its charm and benefits."

Her dedication to book arts grew as her interest in commercial work waned and she pursued a master's degree focusing on papermaking, bookbinding and letterpress printing. Soon after finishing, Jessica moved to the Pacific Northwest where she could set up shop in her garage while also teaching book arts at a local university. A cross-country move with tons of equipment is daunting, but Tacoma has been an amazing place to spend her last 17 years. Her work at Springtide Press–artist books, broadsides, and ephemera–is included in collections around the country and abroad.

Jessica has an abundance of wood and metal type in her collection, which includes ornaments, borders, and a variety of cuts. She has been collecting them for decades, so that makes it easy to amass quite a lot of equipment. "I would compare it to spices in the kitchen—I love a variety of tastes and flavours, so I like to have them all handy. There's never enough space in the shop (or kitchen)."

1. Jessica Spring in her Springtide Press studio.

2. A corner of the print shop.

Collaborations are an important part of Jessica's work, either printing for other artists or teaching traditional letterpress printing, typography, and book arts. She collaborated on the ongoing *Dead Feminists* series and co-authored *Dead Feminists: Historic Heroines in Living Color*. "The opportunity to collaborate with Chandler O'Leary on the *Dead Feminists* project since 2008 has been full of joy and inspiration. Collaboration is also challenging, but the work shows the best of us together: The ideas flow back and forth, we take risks together, and I am constantly learning. I'm incredibly proud of this project and grateful for the historic women who have been collaborators as well," Jessica says.

Jessica has an MFA from Columbia College, Chicago. She teaches workshops virtually and in-person around the country, including Penland, Paper & Book Intensive, Wells Book Arts Institute, Hamilton Wood Type & Printing Museum, and the International Printing Museum. For those who want to pursue letterpress printing, Jessica has advice for them, "Learn the basics first, then defy gravity!"

Get Impressed

◀▲ *Memory Lame* focuses on retention and loss of memory. The book structure must be built by the reader with content emanating from a central, pentagonal memory palace—the most common mnemonic place system—aided by cues of geometric shapes and large numerals. Surrounding the palace are excerpts from *Rhetorica ad Herennium*, the oldest known book on rhetoric and memory.

▶ *Wood* celebrates Hamilton Type Museum's 20th anniversary and was printed with wood and metal type and ornaments.

054

A tree's WOOD is also its MEMOIR

WISE WORDS BY HOPE JAHREN PRINTED FOR HAM AT 20 BY SPRINGTIDE PRESS ○ 2019

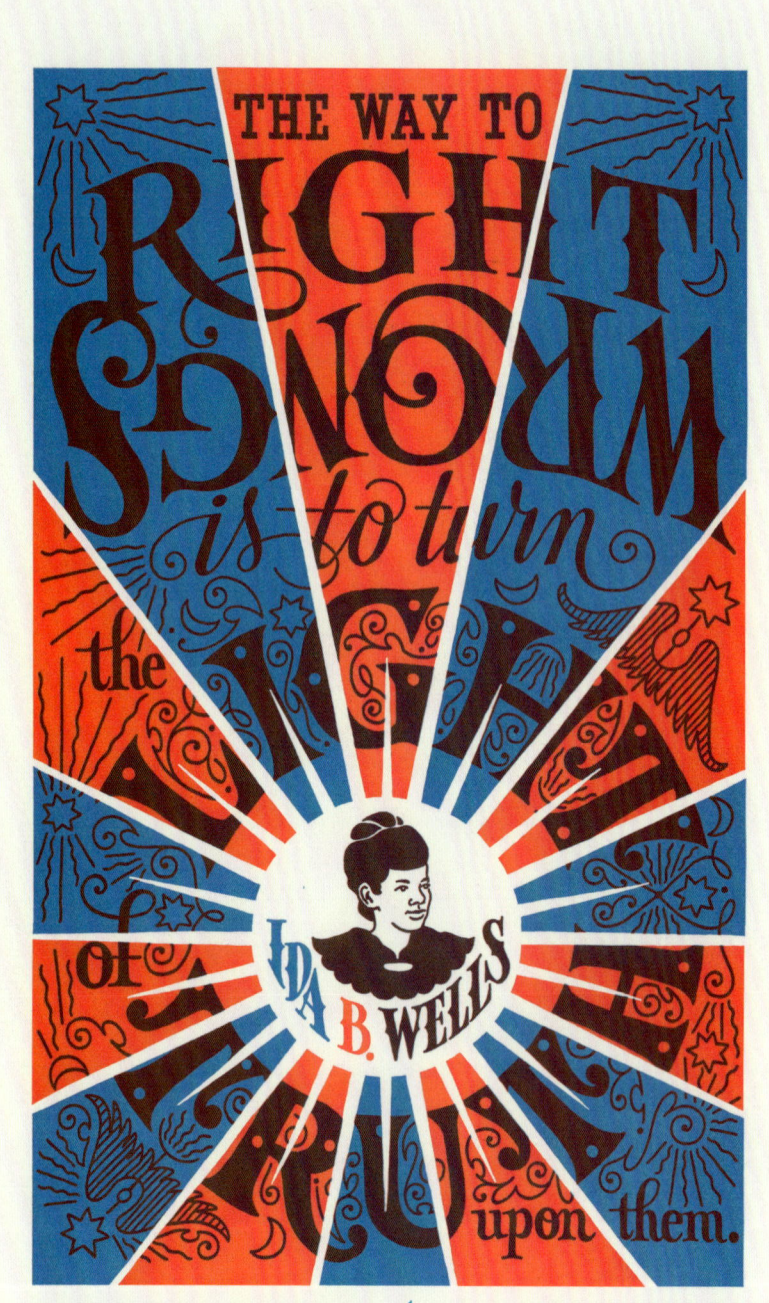

**THE WAY TO RIGHT WRONGS is to turn the LIGHT OF TRUTH upon them.**

**IDA B. WELLS**

Ida Bell Wells-Barnett (1862–1931) was born into slavery in Holly Springs, Mississippi. Her parents and infant brother died in the yellow fever epidemic of 1878, leaving her to care for five siblings. At 21 she moved to Memphis, commuting by train to teach at a rural school. After refusing to give up her purchased seat in a first class car, she was forced off the train. Wells filed and won a lawsuit in 1884, but the state Supreme Court reversed the decision. The experience launched her writing career, and she bought into a small newspaper, the *Free Speech and Headlight*. She began investigating the practice of lynching, calling it "a national crime [requiring] a national remedy." By 1950 more than 4,400 people — most of them Black men, most in the South — were murdered, sometimes witnessed by crowds for entertainment. Wells published pamphlets filled with firsthand accounts and statistics, revealing a relentless regime of terror and oppression. In response, white mobs sent death threats and destroyed her printing press, forcing her to flee Memphis.

Moving north to Chicago, she also became a tireless worker for civil rights and women's suffrage. In 1893 she founded the Women's Era Club, a first-of-its-kind civic club for Black women in Chicago. She also co-founded the Alpha Suffrage Club to focus on expanding voting rights for all women, and co-founded the National Association for the Advancement of Colored People (NAACP). At the 1913 Woman Suffrage Parade in Washington, DC, she and other Black suffragists refused to march in the rear, instead joining white marchers up front. Wells spent the rest of her life advocating for civil rights, equality, and universal suffrage for people of every race, class, and sex. She was awarded a posthumous Pulitzer Prize in 2020, in recognition of her "outstanding and courageous" investigative journalism on lynching. Illustrated by Chandler O'Leary and printed by Jessica Spring, in honor of women who stand at the intersection of feminism and racial justice, interrogating inequality. 193 copies were printed by hand at Springtide Press in Tacoma. May 2020

Letterpress Artists and Printmakers

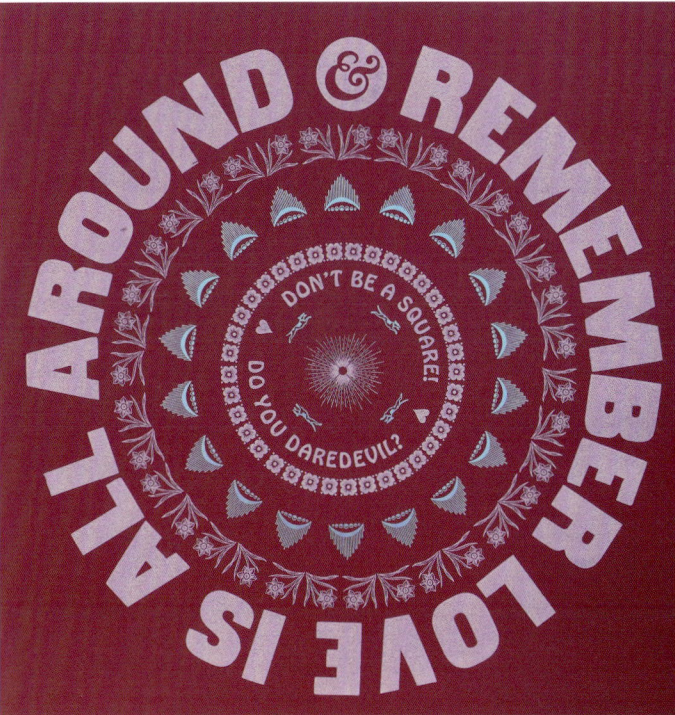

◀ "Truth or Consequences" *Dead Feminists* broadside by Chandler O'Leary and Jessica Spring.

▲ Valentine keepsake using Daredevil Furniture with handset metal type and ornaments with wood type.

▶ Field Notes by Jessica Spring.

**01  How did you get involved in letterpress printing?**

I started typesetting at Macalester College for the weekly student newspaper once I figured out that typesetters got paid while the writers did their work for free. It was challenging work, staying up all night to meet a looming deadline, working on a huge phototypesetting console limited to four typefaces at a time… and those four included the bold and italic. A small green screen showed long lines of code and text which would control every aspect of the type, but nothing was revealed until the photographic paper was developed, typos and all. I confess now that I took advantage of having this equipment at my disposal: While everyone else was pounding away on electric typewriters, my papers were carefully typeset and not one professor noticed generous letter-spacing or line spacing to fulfill their page counts.

After college I continued typesetting, working at one of the last type houses on Printer's Row in Chicago. We digitally composed huge Rand McNally atlas charts that specified which campsites allowed dogs, which had hot showers or flush toilets, all conveyed with tiny icons. The work was challenging, but we had the first WYSIWYG consoles that allowed typesetters to send a preview image to another screen before sending the file out to RC paper—the stuff we used to create mechanical paste-ups. It turns out I had stepped into the beginning of desktop publishing and as I learned on the earliest Apple computers, I also had the chance to learn letterpress printing, moving simultaneously back in typographic history.

# INTERVIEW WITH JESSICA SPRING

**02 How do you visualise an idea into letterpress printing?**

Typically I avoid using the computer and start by sketching ideas. I'll set type, proof with carbon paper then cut those prints up and move things around as needed. Handling the type itself—especially the big wood type—creates a breakthrough. Sometimes the computer is a means for sketching as well, especially for more complex projects. I definitely think of my work as solving a problem, or a puzzle—taking different forms, paper, ink, typefaces and deciding what works together and serves the conceptual idea. Wordplay is usually a critical part of the solution, and what delights me about printing.

**03 What does letterpress mean to you? What kinds of possibilities do you think letterpress contains?**

My work has been a mix of teaching, collaborating, and creating including the *Dead Feminists* broadsides, producing Daredevil Furniture for printers to handset type, and editing artists' books for libraries around the world. Letterpress printing is the opportunity to start with an idea and move it to printing form, whether an artist book or print. The power of taking an idea from conception to printed piece is palpable: I have a voice, but also the means of production. My craft continues to focus on amplifying voices needing to be heard, telling stories in a new way, and ultimately, preservation through production.

**04 Traditional letterpress printing has facing challenges in this digital era. What do you think of this phenomenon?**

I have had so many people ask me about the challenge of working in a "dying trade." I finally had to print a multi-coloured response: "Living is a dying trade." I think the resurgence of letterpress printing is directly related to our digital era: Equipment is easier to find and save; mentors and students can connect more readily; and interest continues to grow with the desire to return to making.

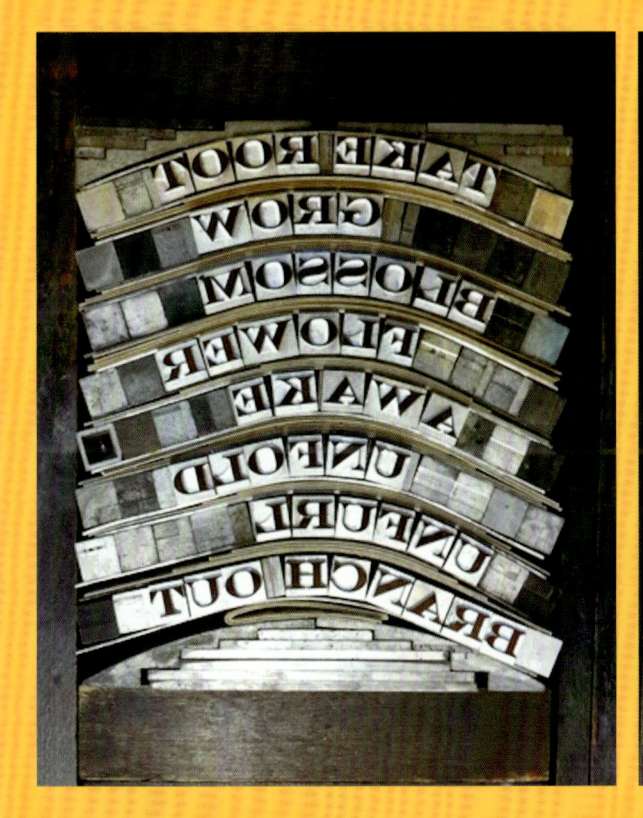

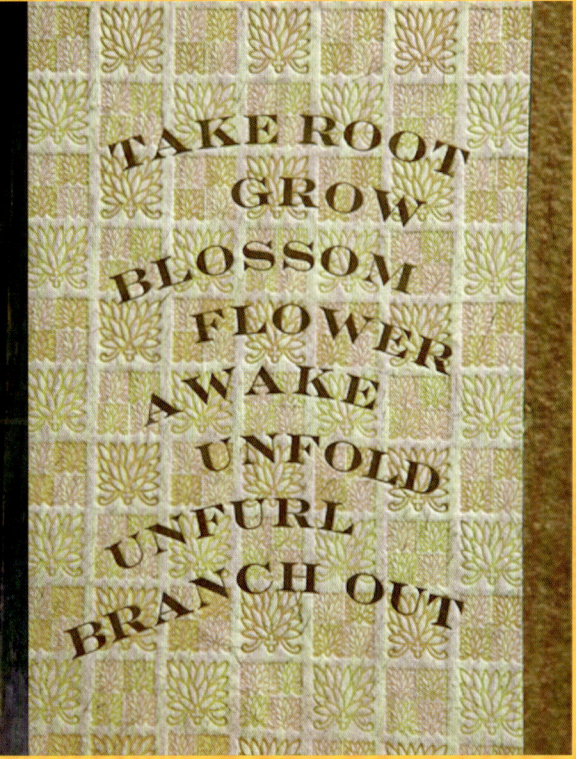

# SHAWN MENDES

SHAWN MENDES ↑ THE TOUR

JULY 20, 2019 ← TULSA, OK → BOK CENTER

"It really opens up opportunities to do good and engage in such a unique way in the 21st century."

# BRAD VETTER

**Louisville, Kentucky, USA**

Brad Vetter is a designer, letterpress printer, artist, and educator currently based in Louisville, Kentucky. Soon after graduating from Western Kentucky University where he studied graphic design and printmaking, Brad began working at the legendary Hatch Show Print in Nashville, Tennessee. At Hatch, he did everything from sweeping the floors to training the interns, all while printing posters for his favourite bands and bringing a fresh new approach to working with the antiquated process of letterpress.

Armed with a Vandercook printing press and some wood type, Brad went on to start his own shop, Brad Vetter Design, in 2012. He took on more digital design projects while never taking off his printing apron. Working between analog and digital, Brad's prints are created with a combination of antique types or presses and a state-of-the-art laser engraver. Now residing in Louisville, Brad spends his time teaching workshops, designing fun things, printing letterpress show posters (for Chris Stapleton, Margo Price, and the late John Prine, to name a few), building community, and occasionally making art.

Brad's designs often manipulate the antique type into something that does not easily translate back into traditional letterpress. This is where a laser engraver comes in. He uses the laser to create new printing blocks to work from. "This tool is never a replacement for the type and imagery I have in my collection; one of my favourite things is the potential to create type that is dropped out of a larger background. This

1. Brad Vetter and his poster wall.
2. Printing tools.

allows me to fill the page with colour while still holding to the integrity of the antique type." He has always been drawn to the imperfections in letterpress—the way that scratches and dents in his wood type, or the inconsistency of something that is hand-inked. "That is what I find so fascinating about the process, the fact that it is made by a person." Brad says.

For Brad, people and stories are important in his work. Brad has designed for lots of music artists and events. He always starts with playing some music because he wants to feel connected to the band, to the songs they are writing, and how any of that may translate into the aesthetic of the poster he is about to design. "I have always loved music, but could never play. Getting to work with musicians to design record covers and posters is an opportunity for me to be a part of the culture of music in America. When the purpose of poster printing shifted from advertising to more of a work of art, it allowed us to focus less on making sure that the information is legible, to making a print that celebrates the musicians, their fans and music."

Usually, Brad starts from a place of conversation and collaboration with the client. If the client is a musician, he would spend time listening to their music and getting a real understanding of what the poster should look and feel like. Then he may sketch down the idea on paper, "I only start setting type or designing on the computer once I have a pretty solid idea or concept or composition."

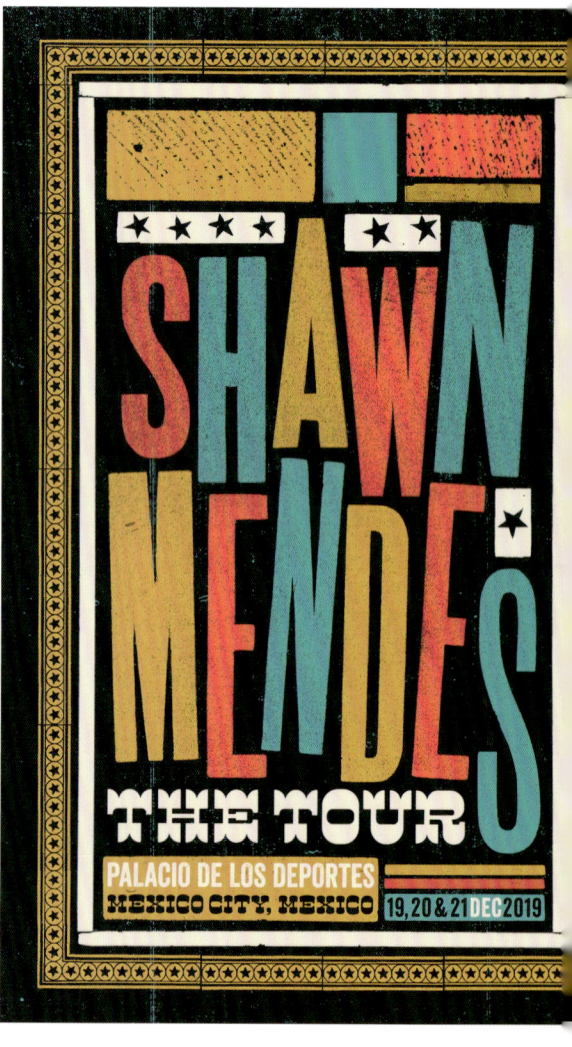

▲ **Shawn Mendes The Tour**

The crew for Shawn Mendes reached out to Brad Vetter to see if he would be able to design a poster for each show that Shawn would be playing on his 2019 world tour. These posters were all designed digitally (from scanned letterpress elements) for Instagram stories. In total, Brad designed over 75 unique posters. The posters were mostly used for marketing, but they were also sold at the shows and became a huge mural outside a few bigger shows as a place for fans to take pictures.

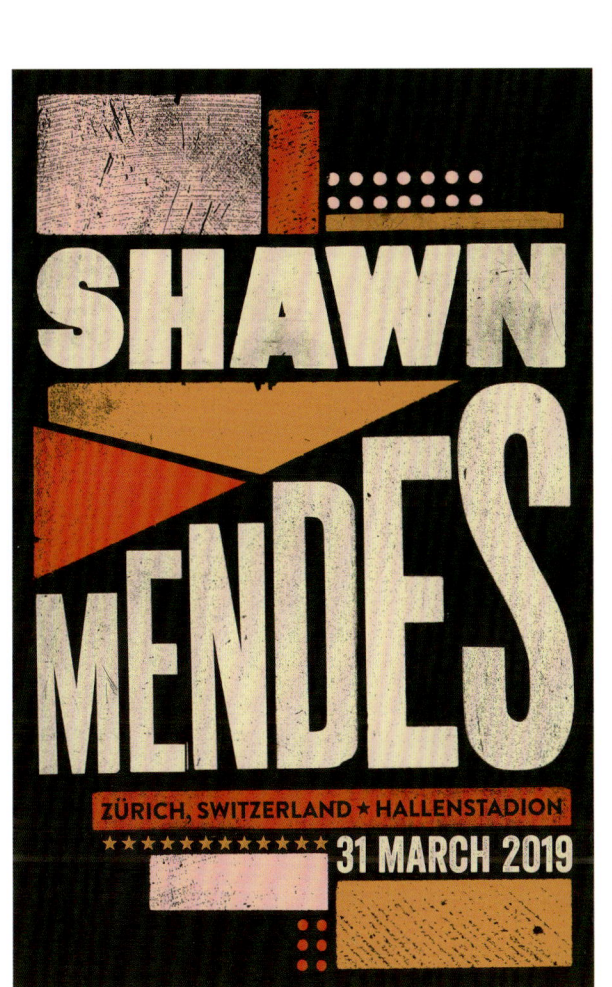

Hand-set wood type and a few other digital faces were used in the design. Brad Vetter began the project by typesetting "Shawn Mendes The Tour" and a bunch of figures and other hand-printed elements with a large variety of typefaces.

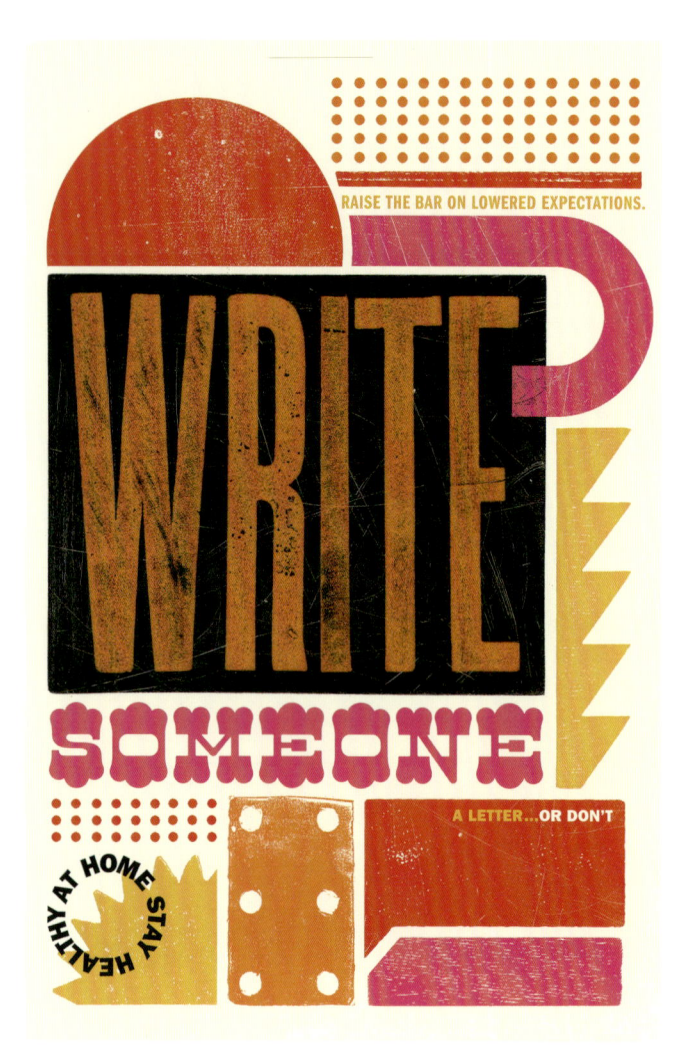

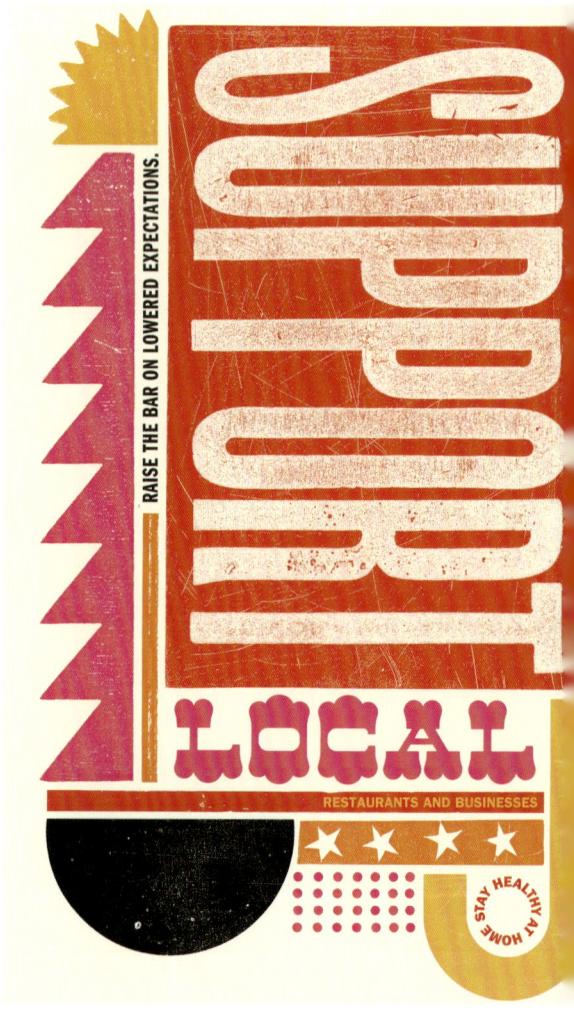

▲ Erase Covid

Brad was asked to design some PSA style posters for a project called Erase Covid to both raise awareness on the steps people should be taking to fight Covid-19, but also to benefit some organisations affected by the virus. The project featured poster artists from around the US.

▲ **Ham @ 20**

As Hamilton Wood Type and Printing Museum's Artist in Residence, Jen Farrell (of Starshaped Press) invited several letterpress artists to contribute a poster celebrating what the museum means to everyone. Hamilton means so much to so many letterpress printers for the education, preservation and the people who are there to celebrate, preserve, listen and tell the stories of letterpress printing. Brad wanted to make a design that paid homage to the history of letterpress as well as the amazing community the process inspires.

# INTERVIEW WITH BRAD VETTER

**01 You create antique types in both analog and digital. Why do you choose to work in this style? Could you share with us your working process?**

I love bouncing between digital and analog. I never see one overpowering the other. I think it is a totally symbiotic relationship; both are necessary to create the images I am printing. Once I have an idea for a design, I start pulling type that feels relevant to the client and composition. After proofing the type on the letterpress, I will scan letterpress elements and start to manipulate these images digitally if needed, or just play around with colour and composition. The digital file makes it easy to communicate with the client what the final design will approximately look like.

**02 How do you keep the history of letterpress relevant in a world of modern technology?**

I have never been overly wrapped up in the history of letterpress. I came to the process through my love of music and concert posters. When I was younger and going to shows a lot, I remember walking down the street and seeing posters stapled to the telephone poles or pasted to walls. That was how I learned who was coming to town and even a bit about the culture that surrounded music. I was always drawn to that aesthetic and how it became a part of my everyday life. These days, posters aren't used quite as often to advertise a concert on the streets, but typically sold as a merchandise item at the show. I love this new challenge of engaging and interacting with my community through this antique form of printing. It's funny how we spend so much time hand-setting type and printing "the old way" so that we can take a photo of that work to put onto the Internet. I am less interested in the way that we can reach a larger audience, and more excited about the potential of creating meaningful interaction between the viewer and my work. The technologies help create the aesthetic and speed of my work that may change the context of seeing a poster in the wild. Maybe instead of seeing the work on a telephone pole, the posters may be seen as a mural outside a stadium concert, or a bottle of wine on the shelf at the liquor store, or artwork that lives in public spaces where anyone and everyone can view and engage with a piece of letterpress work.

**03 You strive to push letterpress forward and explore its possibilities. What kinds of possibilities do you think letterpress contains?**

There is a line that says "Freedom of the press is guaranteed only to those who own one." I have always loved this line. There is a responsibility to letterpress. It's so much more than just putting ink on paper. It's about sharing ideas and reaching for what is right and just in the world. We all have different voices, some are louder than others. I hope that I can use my press—and this process—to raise those voices that need raising, and continue to share my knowledge of letterpress with as many folks as possible, with the hopes that they too can continue the traditions and history of the printed word.

**04 You have worked with rock star clientele and musicians, such as Chris Stapleton, Mumford & Sons, and Shawn Mendes. What will you take into consideration when working with these artists?**

When I started working at Hatch Show Print (140+ year-old letterpress shop in Nashville), I was getting to make posters for a lot of bands I had loved forever. Getting to work with Wilco was huge for me at the time, and it still is. The posters we were making then—and are still being made by the amazing designers and printers there today—still hung in the shadows of the beautiful prints made in the late 1800s into the mid-1900s celebrating the entertainers and musicians of that time. It was always so incredible to me that I could be using the same wood type "C" to set a poster for the Counting Crows in 2005, that was maybe used to make a poster for Johnny Cash in 1965. The history of Hatch was so tied to the history of entertainment in the American South.

To me, these artists are working their hardest to make the best sounds that they can. Maybe it came easy to some of them, but they are still hard-working creatives. I try to keep that in mind when I am making these prints. I will push the capabilities and traditions of letterpress with the hopes of creating something that feels meaningful and celebratory of their music. This is equally true for the lesser-known artists as well. I almost think most of those posters are better than the big names—there is less pressure, and usually less client feedback allowing me to make something more authentic for these indie musicians. Either way, whenever I work on these projects, I know that my audience is not the band at all, but the fans, and those are the folks I am trying to impress.

STRANGE HOTELS
FINNEAS
DECEMBER TO REMEMBER
CRYSTAL BALLROOM
PORTLAND OR
ABC
CMYK

"Imperfection allows me freedom when I work, but that doesn't mean I don't strive for perfection. I will embrace it when it happens and then try to control that process back into the print."

# CHRIS CHANDLER

**Portland, Oregon, USA**

Before stepping into letterpress printing, Chris Chandler experimented with pottery and photography and struggled with waiting to see the results. "With pottery and photography you wait for your work to come back from the kiln and the film to get developed at the lab, but with printing you see the results as you go and can adjust on the spot. I love this immediacy of working." He was first introduced to letterpress in Los Angeles in the mid-90s by Bruce Licher, the owner of Independent Project Press. At that time, Chris was in a band, "Our band shared a rehearsal space and I was intrigued by his prints on the wall. It was Bruce who encouraged me to get my first press. At that time it was a means for me to create promotional posters and flyers for the band I played in, but it grew into my own creative art practice as time went on."

In 1996, he founded Neu Haus Press when he acquired his first Vandercook press in Venice Beach, California. Through the years his love, talent, knowledge, and collection of this vintage craft has grown. In talking about his process, Chris says, "My first consideration is usually asking myself: Where it is going to go? Am I making a wheat-pasted mural outside or a smaller work to be framed or mounted on a panel? I am guided by what paper I am drawn to, what blocks I want to use or custom make for a specific work. Honestly though, most of my considerations come with the process of the printing. I will put down the first few colours, go home and sleep on it, come back in a day or two and add the remaining colours, go home and sleep on it, repeat until I decide it is done."

1-2. Chris Chandler and his Neu Haus Press. Photos by Airyka Rockefeller and Evan Beasley.

072

From 30 years working as a tour manager and sound engineer for bands, Chris has had the privilege to share his passion to letterpress with musicians through collaborations with their artwork. Chris also tries to combine music with letterpress. Music has been such a defining thing in his life—"from seeing drum patterns and scores in my prints to my Fade-Out prints referencing 'fading out' while working in a recording studio or even making posters for concerts." He balanced music and art for about 20 years with traveling, touring, recording, managing and making prints. Now, he is enjoying dedicating more time to the print studio, where music is constantly filling his work space and keeping his flow going.

Residing in Portland, Chris is able to expand his printing portfolio and create letterpress art. He was inspired by pioneers of graphic design such as master typographer Jan Tschichold, El Lissitzky, and the Expressionist painter and printmaker Erich Heckel. He now partners with Hannah Bakken. Hannah hails from Malheur County, Oregon and works interdisciplinarity by combining printed media with performance, sculpture, and installation to explore identity, the body, landscape, and place. She is the studio manager of Neu Haus Press.

▲ In 1944, American Type Founders (ATF) introduced Alpha-Blox, an impressive system of both solid and linear shapes that could be combined to create all manners of typefaces, ornaments and pattern in one or two colours. Chris recreated and re-envisioned the font in large wood block form. Printing on his Vandercook 232P and with the assistance of Max Collins's use of wheat paste as an adhesive, Chris has created billboards as large as 14' × 20'.

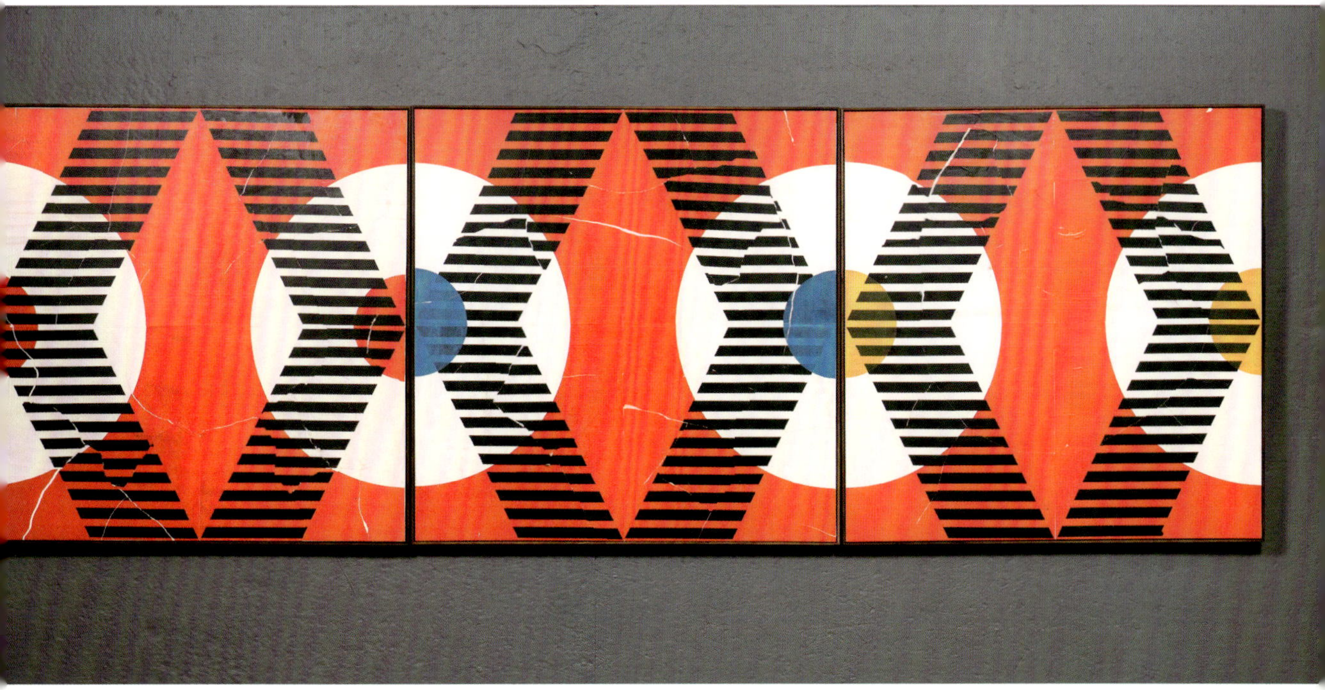

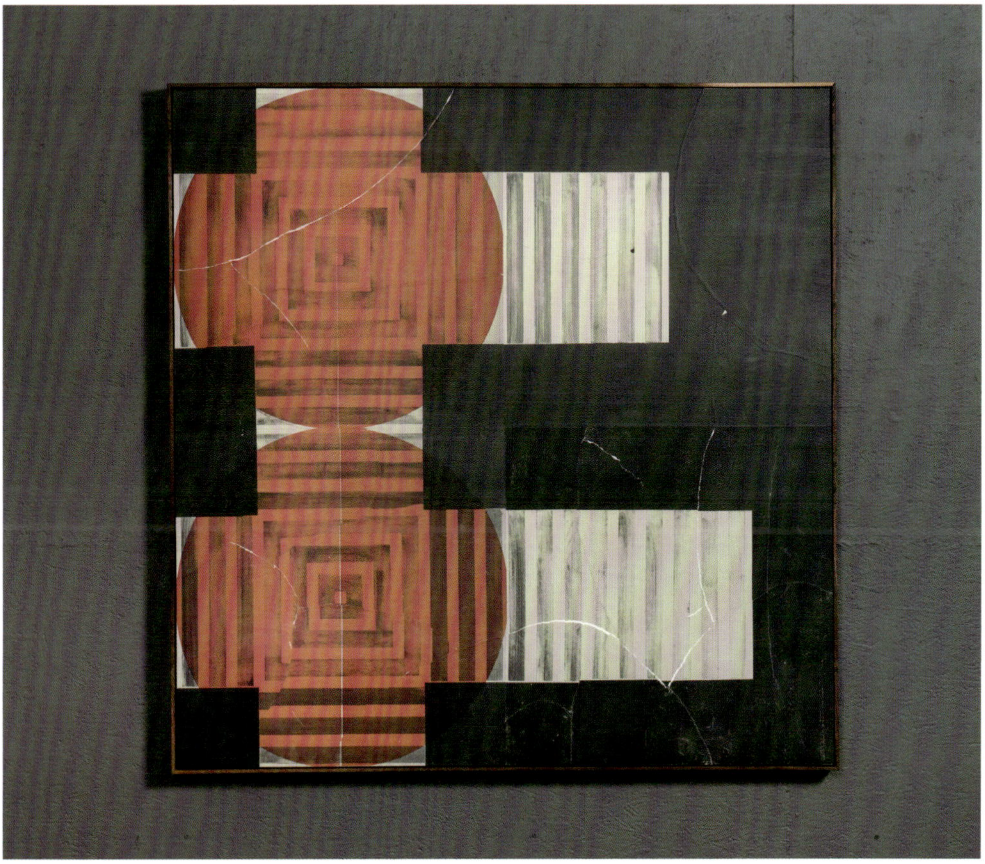

▲ ▶ Linear-Reverse exhibits large-scale relief monoprint works by Chris Chandler of Neu Haus Press. Chris uses the lexicon of his large-scale Alpha-Blox to plan his overall compositions and patterns, yet allows for freedom in his layering of colours, dimensional play through wood grains, and visual reveals of colour and texture from wheatpasting the prints to panel surfaces. The resulting works focus on beauty and simplicity in design, visual associations within abstraction, and the endless possibilities of working iteratively within a modular system.

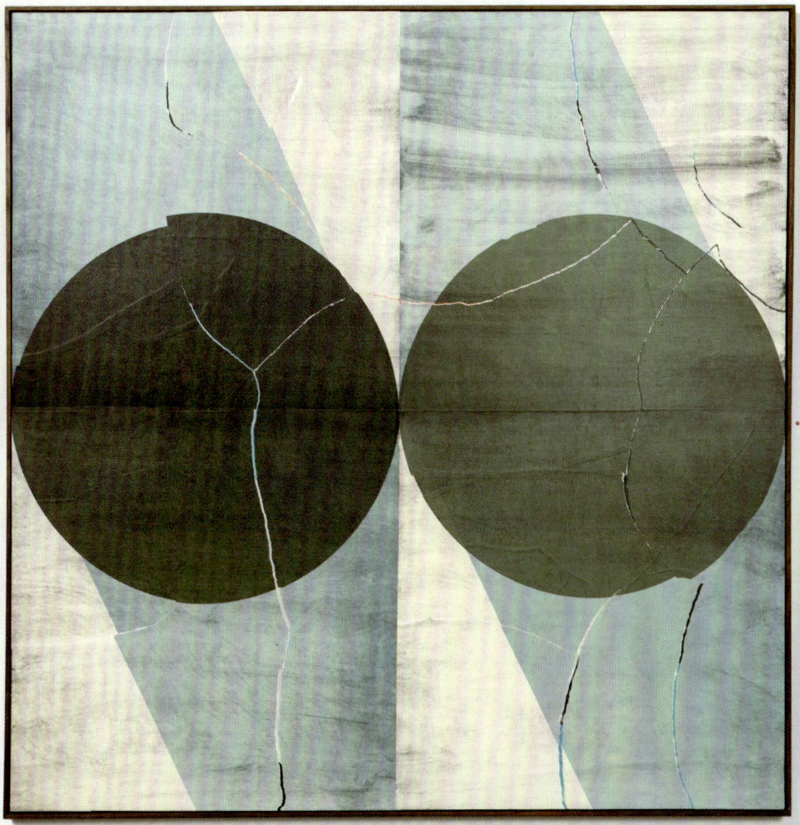

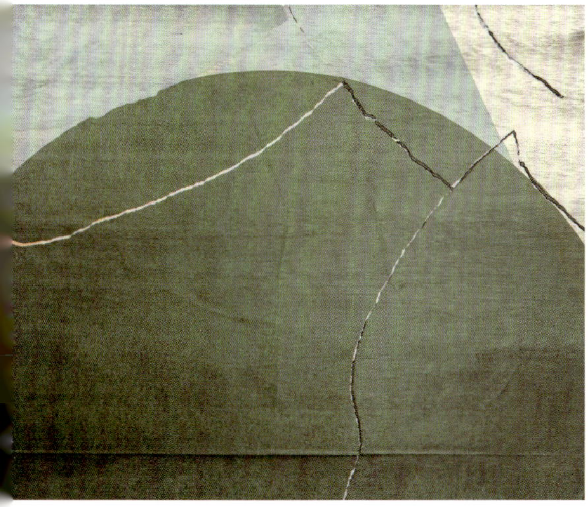

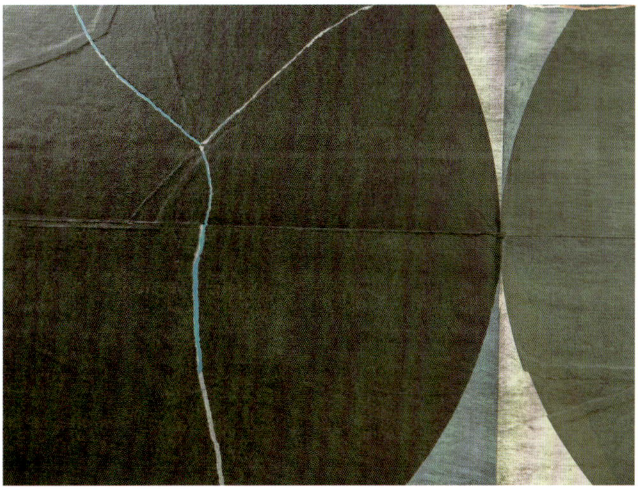

▲ Linear-Reverse highlights the importance of Chris's creative process, and the collaborative dynamic between him and his Vandercook press. He simultaneously works within the confines of the Alpha-Blox design and the freedom of monoprinting, creating a body of work where each piece is individualised and is a record of the constructive conflict between artist and machine. Chris's creativity showcases the beauty that results from the reproductive nature of working within analogue print processes.

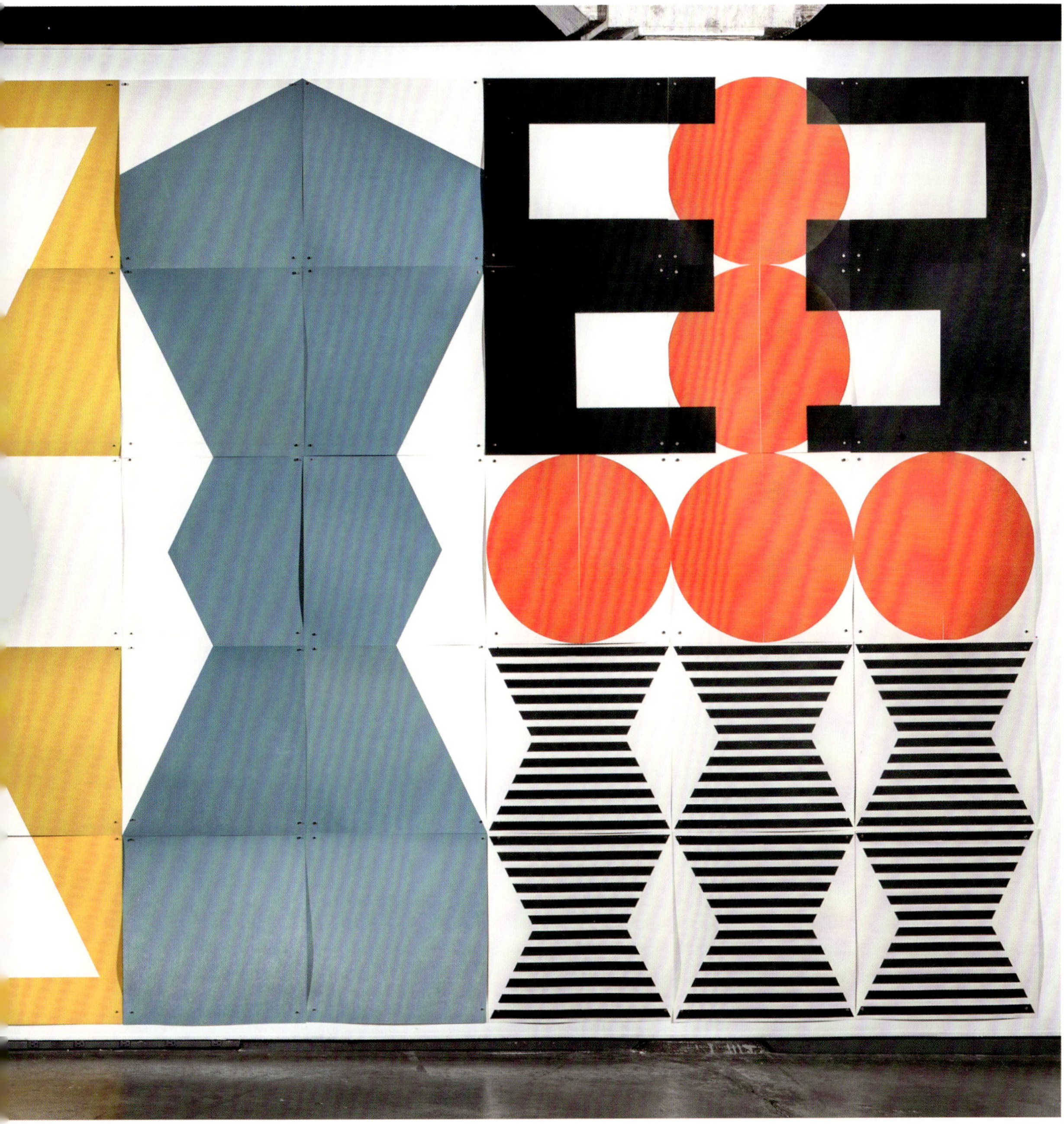

*01 Your printing isn't controlled in terms of the method—the unexpected and imperfections matter more in your works. What does "imperfection" mean to you?*

I feel that I do actually have a very controlled method of production that comes from noticing moments of imperfection in what I make. When I was younger, I had a perfect, brand-new guitar that I was afraid to touch and use. However, after my brother dropped it, I felt freed to use it and like the stakes weren't as high anymore. I feel like my way of working goes back to moments like those in my youth. Imperfection allows me freedom when I work, but that doesn't mean I don't strive for perfection. I will embrace it when it happens and then try to control that process back into the print.

*02 Colours and geometric graphics take the lead in your works. What's your colour scheme or design philosophy?*

Usually, my design philosophy is centered around "less is more" and using repetition in a way that allows for difference and shifts in the patterns I use in my woodblocks. I would say my colour schemes change with each print until I find what I like for each one. Lately, I have been drawn to working first with a flat colour for the first layer of ink, usually a cream with an aged look. These flats give a layer of dimension to the print that I hadn't achieved before by just printing my compositions straight onto the paper.

*03 How do you describe your own style?*

I bounce a lot of ideas off of my father, who is also an artist. He and I talk about our own term "Art-Mecanica": you have to be a mechanic to keep your presses running, constantly fixing and repairing them, and also these machines can dictate your style and process. So there is always a machine and artist working together to create. I would describe my art style as this: I am a person using this massive tool to make my art and that molds the style that is present in my work.

# INTERVIEW WITH CHRIS CHANDLER

**04 As a sound engineer, you are known for sticking with analog tapes and consoles rather than moving to the digital world. Why?**

As a sound engineer, I was known for sticking with the analog tapes and consoles rather than moving to the digital world. I find the same to be true in my art, using "analog" machines from the 20's through the 50's. From the maintenance and restoration of these machines to the design and printing, I find that I'm more connected to the pieces of the process, not just the results. I embrace the limitations of analog like only having 24 tracks to make a statement instead of endless digital options. Analog printing functions similarly. You have to make intentional decisions and can't get overwhelmed by endless possibilities.

**05 You've held several events and exhibitions. The recent exhibition, Linear–Reverse, has received lots of attention. Could you tell us more about it?**

That show was in Oklahoma City, my home away from home where I spent a lot of time with the Flaming Lips and I was happy to go back there for a show. The exhibition opened right when Covid-19 hit, so the space was only open for a couple of days before it had to close. The gallery put together a virtual show which I am grateful for. It was huge that people were able to see it from all over the world and not have to be in OKC to see it. It was nice to be back in Oklahoma City as a print artist and not a working tour manager. This was my biggest solo exhibition and it was a great experience to see everything together in one space along with a big mural which is always fun for me.

# things

7049
200 g/m²
Golden yellow

"The small imperfections, the greasy ink, and the beautiful paper made me want to learn more about it."

# BART HEESEN

**Helden, The Netherlands**

1-4. Bart Heesen in Karakter Prints.

**B**art Heesen started Karakter Prints (Karakter is the Dutch name for "character", referring to both the character of imperfect printing and the letters Bart works with) as a hobby after he had a letterpress birth announcement printed for his son. He was so impressed with the end result that he started teaching himself this technique. First, he practised all at the kitchen table, but soon larger presses followed.

In 2014, Bart decided to start Karakter Prints. In the years that followed, Karakter Prints developed into a versatile studio in which stamps and letterpress printing form the majority of its work. Karakter Prints is based on a commercial analog printing company. Part of it is a webshop where hand stamps are made and sold. In the Netherlands, it is a tradition to send birth announcements. This is what Bart mainly focuses on in addition to his free work and printing for business. Letterpress gives the birth announcement a special look and feel. For the designs, he makes his own style and he works with some cool designers throughout the country.

In addition, Bart uses elements from the old-fashioned printing technique for creative applications in business and education. Before working full time for himself, he was a social worker. He now combines the best of both worlds in the workshops that he gives to children in schools. Here he works with stamps, block letters and other materials. The workshops go beyond experiencing his most beautiful works. They are also a means to discuss various themes such as self-confidence, cooperation and communication.

Talking about his usual process of designing and producing, Bart says, "I consider myself more of a maker or a creator than a designer. The Netherlands has a tradition of sending announcements after the birth of a child. These cards make up most of my portfolio. In terms of design, I have a fairly raw style. I prefer to work with drawings, both analog or on iPad. I then digitise this. I also work with other illustrators. I dare to focus more and more on this rawer style of design. I think this fits well with letterpress and suits me more. For me, it gives me more pleasure than printing the sugar-sweet birth announcements."

During his unique way of traversing the printing process, despite a wide range of finishing options, people will not encounter many bells and whistles. At Karakter Prints, he prefers to keep it simple. He works with machines between 40 and 125 years old, supplemented with modern techniques such as a laser. All printing presses are operated by hand, meaning that literally every printed card or stamp is made and checked by Bart.

Bart works in a simple style. He shares with us his aesthetic. "When I started I wanted to learn to master all finishing techniques. Although I have mastered them more or less, I now choose to go back to the basics: prints in one or two colours, with appropriate paper, in combination with a strong design. I sometimes use a laser to make shapes in the paper."

Bart has started the Tintenkillers projects together with a collage artist, Rob Benders. As a collective, they make live art in festivals and public places. Moreover, they use elements from collage art and letterpress technique to work with teams and organisations on communication purposes and team building. This out-of-the-box method provides surprising results.

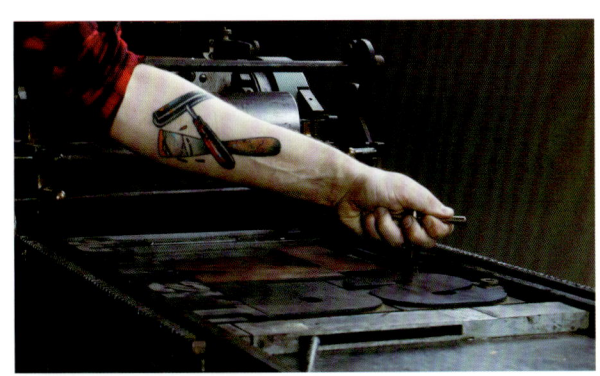

Get Impressed

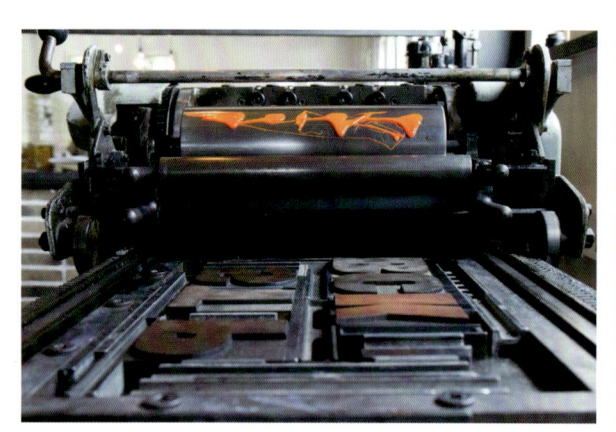

◀▲ In this Print Collage project, Bart used a cutout of a Tintenkillers collage and converted it to a grid. This grid was lasered from a wooden plate before he started printing over this grid again. The 30 prints that followed are currently still printed and pasted as part of an ongoing project. This will create 30 different works.

▲ Lttrprints is a collaboration between Judith Nieken (Lttrvreters) and Karakter Prints. Judith's texts are printed in the studio at Karakter Prints.

▶ Tintenkillers project.

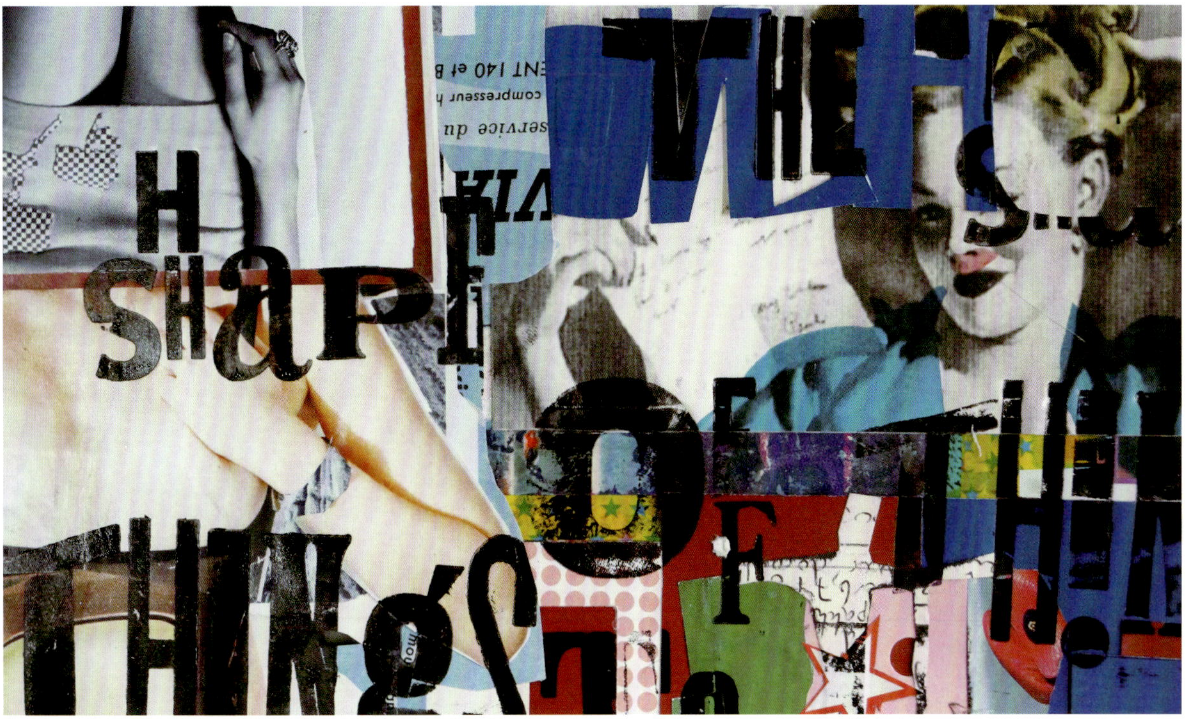
SHAP
THE
OF
THIN

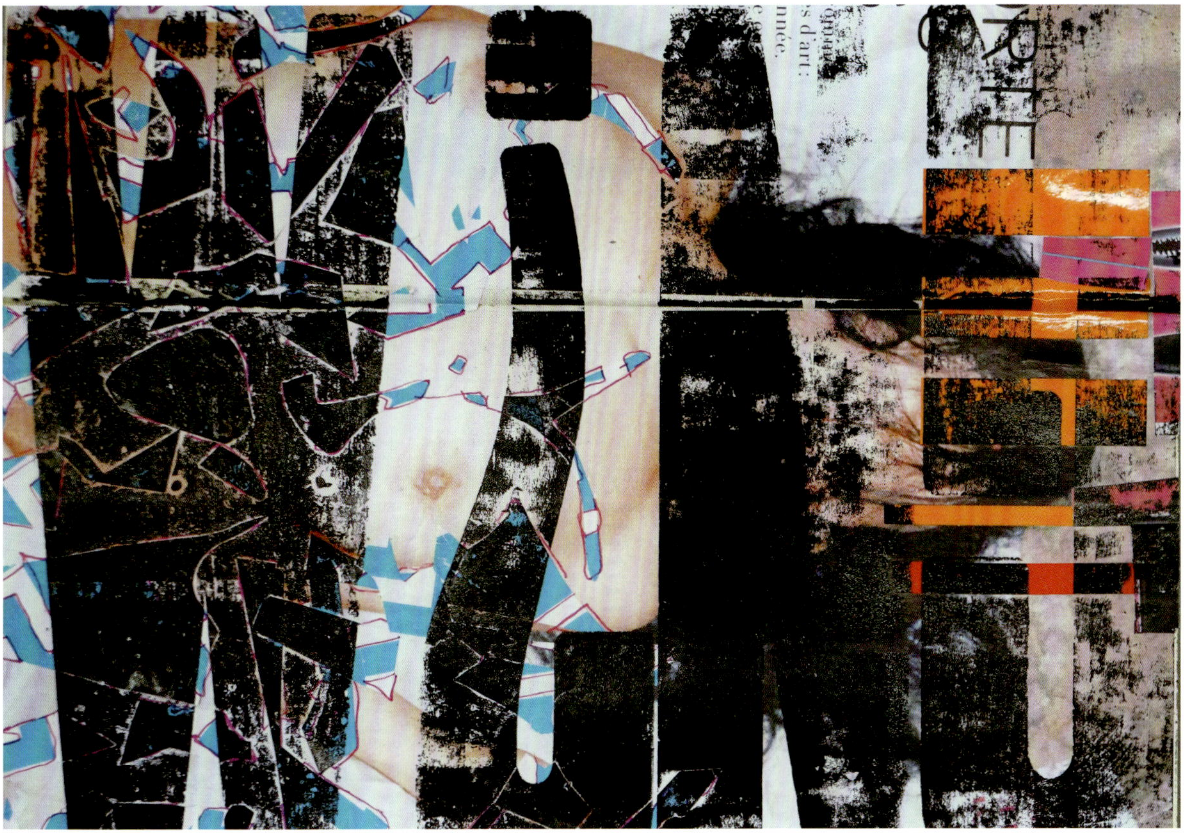

▶ Tintenkillers combines collage art, stamps and letterpress techniques. For the collages, Bart uses leftovers and makeready prints out of the letterpress process.

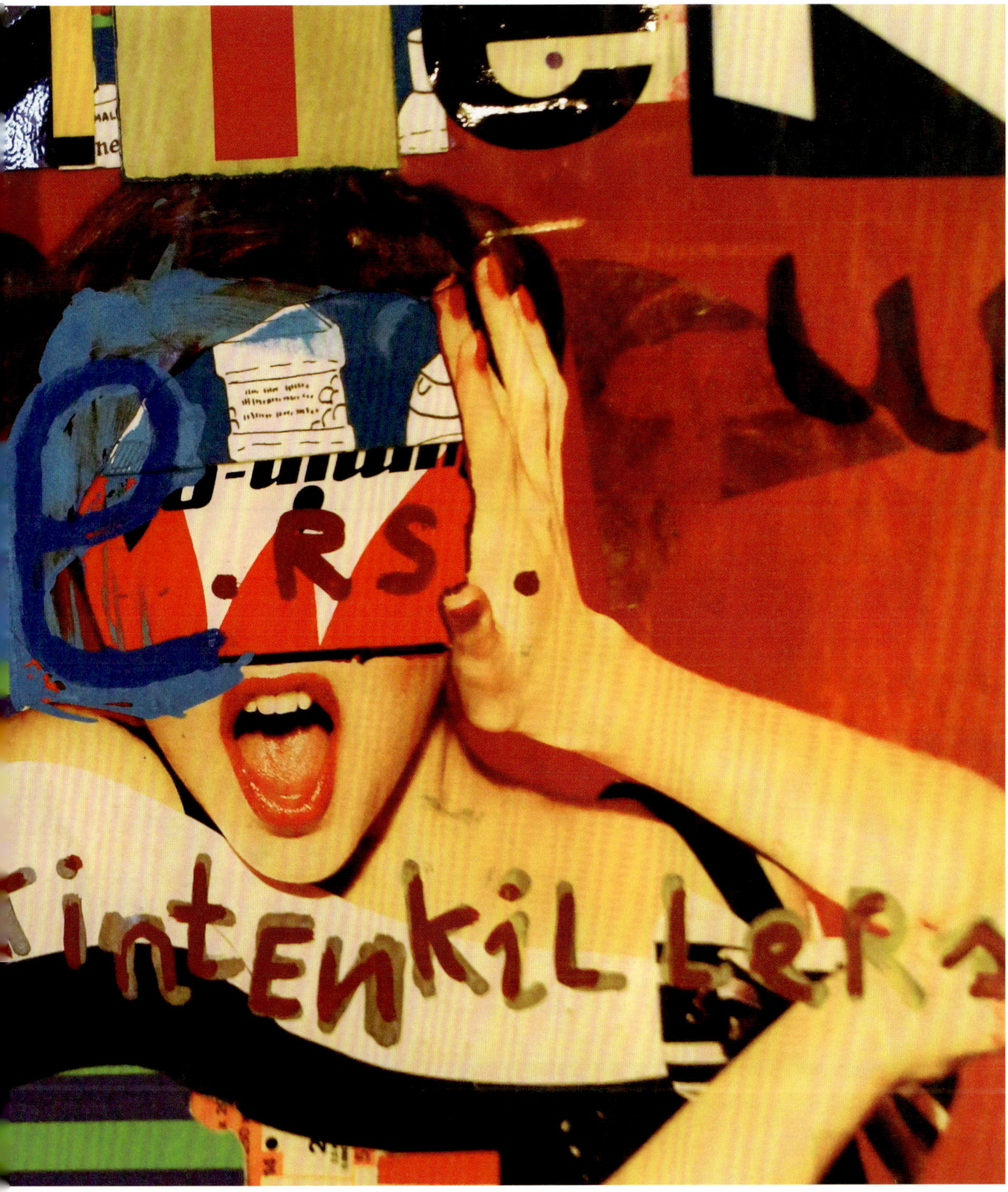

# INTERVIEW WITH BART HEESEN

**01  Seems like you're self-taught in letterpress printing. How did you get involved in this technique?**

I came into contact with letterpress after having my son's birth announcement letterpress printed. I knew I was looking for this style of printing, but at the time I didn't know that this was called letterpress. After I got the cards home it never let go. The small imperfections, the greasy ink, and the beautiful paper made me want to learn more about it. I came into contact with a retired printer who showed me how the technique worked on a small Adana 8 x 5 that I was able to take over somewhere in exchange for a bottle of wine. Soon after, I found a platen press and proofing press. I then worked to master the technique next to my day job in mental health care. This literally cost me blood, sweat and tears. In my case, blood, sweat, and broken fingers, after I once got my hand caught between the platen presses.

**02  Your works discussed self-confidence, cooperation, communication, etc. Why?**

This question is about my workshops. I ended up in the education and museum world when I was asked to give a letterpress workshop in primary school. Since I worked in mental healthcare for 12 years, I quickly saw the potential to use letterpress as a safe and creative way to work and interact with kids and adults, discussing and exploring certain themes or problems. In the meantime, I have devised various programs in which children work on self-confidence, language skills, communication, and other themes. All these are designed with stamps, wooden letters, collage arts, old copy machines, and a lot of ink. I now write programs for schools and museums and work together with a collage artist on the Tintenkillers project, where we work for companies, government, schools and individuals.

**03 You make birth announcements as well as collage print. What's the difference between these projects? What will you take into consideration when working on various projects?**

If you put my birth announcements and collages next to each other you wouldn't be able to recognise a signature. I think this suits me. I've never been able to focus on one thing for a long time. Because of the diversity of activities, I roll from one thing to the other, literally. When I look back on the past years, I have always been given opportunities and collaborations that I previously never thought possible. Because I have to pay the bills with my letterpress work, I often work on an assignment, so I have little time for my own project. I always stay true to myself. Of course, there are sometimes assignments that do not suit me that well, but if something really doesn't suit me, I will express this to a customer. When you make something, you quickly spend a day or more on it. Since I only work on proof presses, each card passes through my hands several times. If it is a product that does not suit you, you cannot make it with passion.

**04 Do you have any advice for those who want to pursue letterpress?**

1. Unscrew everything! I once loosened all the screws on my press. Since I am not technical, I was always afraid of the printing presses. There was no going back then and so I got to know the function of each screw.

2. Get started! It is as simple as it sounds! Letterpress is a technique that excels in its simplicity. It is therefore not that you need much. With a simple press and a few jars of ink, you can get up and running. I am glad I started on an Adana one day. Because I learned to print reasonably on that machine, the other presses

became understandable. A printing press is pretty straightforward. When you turn something, you notice what this does. In the beginning, you can have polymer plates made and borrow other materials somewhere. I bought my first cans of ink based on orders. When a customer needed green, I bought a can. That's how I built everything up.

At the moment, I'm moving my studio back home. I rented a fantastic place in an old factory, but I didn't touch most of my stuff. I sold more than half of my gear and continue working with only two presses and some small gears.

# 04

**Letterpress Factories, Initiatives, Museums, etc.**

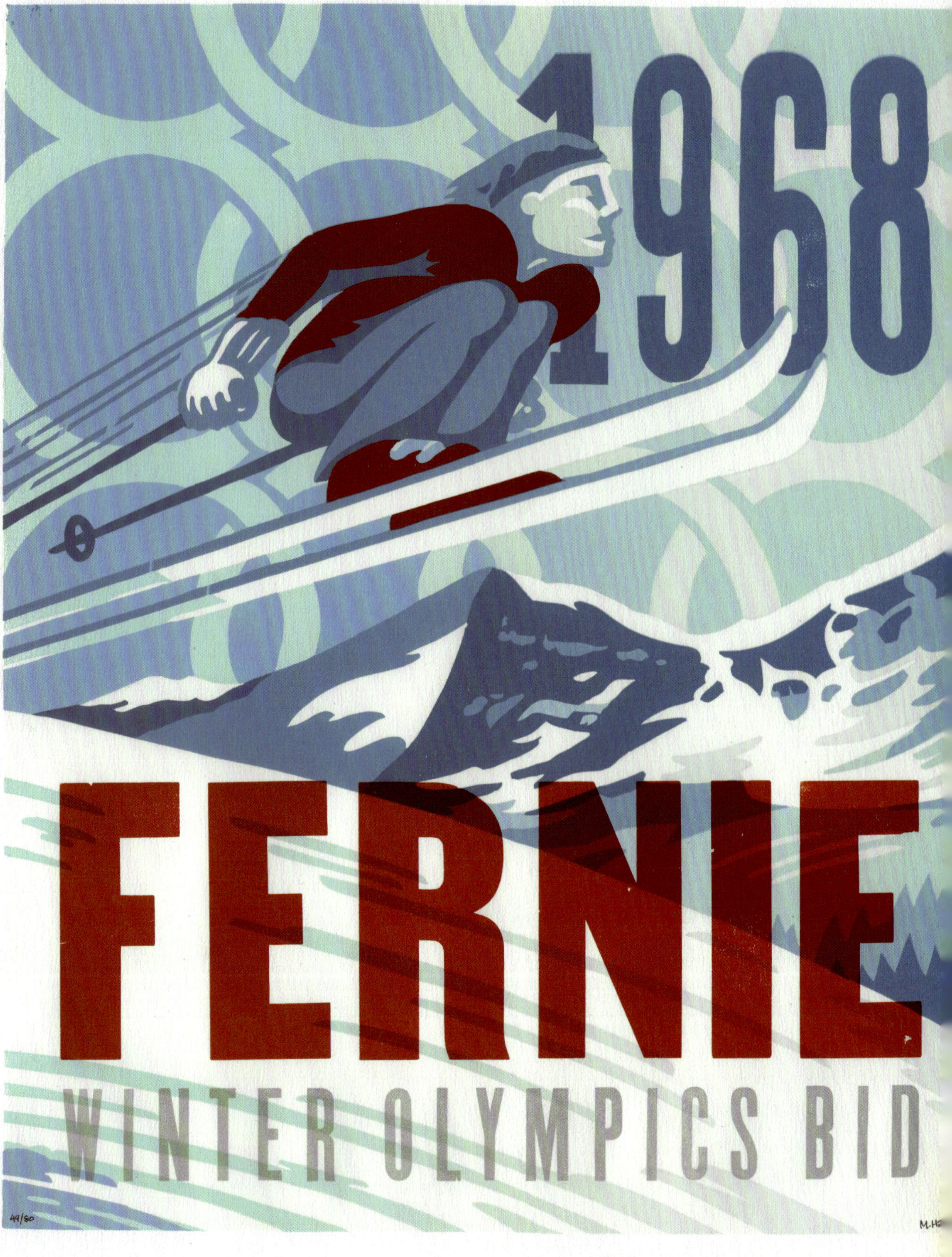
1968
FERNIE
WINTER OLYMPICS BID
49/80

"Printing on letterpress is all about being guided by the limitations. Many of these limits are physical and must be respected, so it's about finding a way to create something that fits within the boundaries but fulfills your vision."

# CLAWHAMMER PRESS

**British Columbia, Canada**

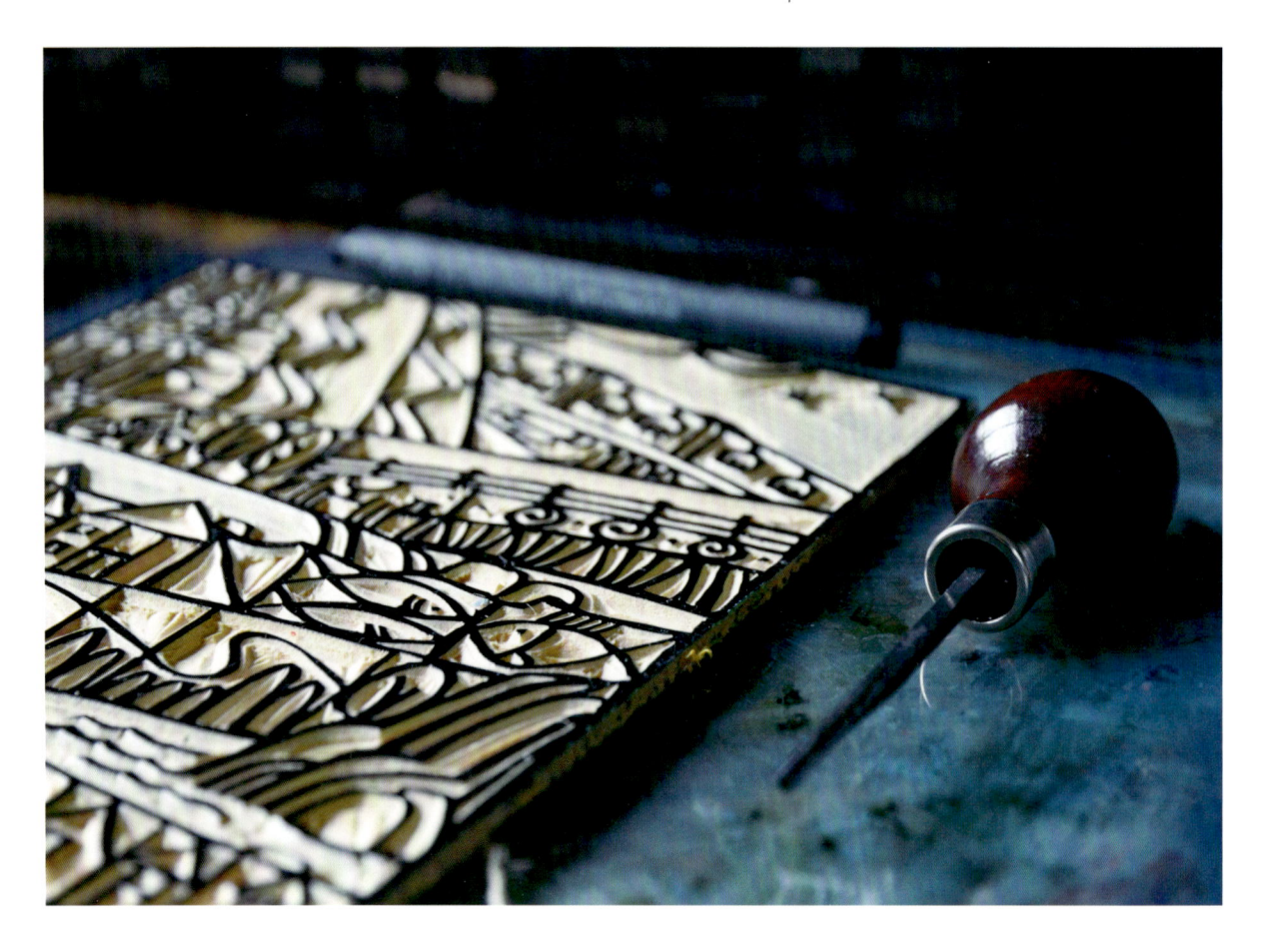

Michael Hepher, the owner and artist behind Clawhammer Press, has a knack for the niche arts. He got involved in letterpress accidentally. Having always been an artisan, Michael works in music, graphic arts and fine arts. In 2001, he apprenticed as an artist-blacksmith, gaining an appreciation for the historic trades. In 2003, he moved back into the digital realm, but he realised that he missed the hands-on connection to work. He thought there might be a way to blend his love for the tactile arts with the love for typography.

Michael happened to find a vintage Chandler & Price and a leather-bound Platen Press Operation book during his visit to a local printer. That's how he learned his way through letterpress printing and fell in love with the process, the machines and the printed results. In the beginning, he had to alter his artistic and creative styles to match the limitations of a printing press, but that was part of the fun of it. "Trained in illustration, there were a lot of skills that parlayed well into designing for a press, but some limitations to work around. On the press, it's all wood block or wooden carving, those are the processes I use, which are reductive rather than additive, so it's more akin to sculpture than it is to drawing, because you are actually carving away the bits that you don't want printed." Michael says.

In 2011, Michael moved to Fernie to launch Clawhammer Press, a working studio and fine art gallery. It is his transition to becoming a full-time printer and fine art printmaker. Clawhammer Press celebrates its 10th anniversary in 2021.

1. Carving session.

2-3. Champagne Powder print.

Clawhammer Press is one of few letterpress shops in Western Canada. It offers full design services, letterpress printing, as well as retail paper products and fine art. Working largely in fine-art prints and ephemeral paper goods that integrate hand-carved blocks, typography, and a slightly off-beat sense of humour, Michael uses a variety of processes to get ink on paper. "I find inspiration all around me: outside, through colleagues' work, friends, books, and historical work. I have a growing collection of prints from around the world that continue to inspire and challenge me," he continues, "Letterpress to me has been like finding a home, a community, a calling, and a voice all in one process. I can't imagine my life without my press, my type, and my printer friends surrounding and inspiring me."

Clawhammer Press holds a variety of workshops, covering everything from basic typesetting, advanced typesetting in metal and wood type, as well as lino block and woodblock printing. The artists are happy to present guest lecturers or remote seminars to help grow the knowledge of the letterpress in Western Canada. They also do private local or remote workshops and seminars, and events for school groups.

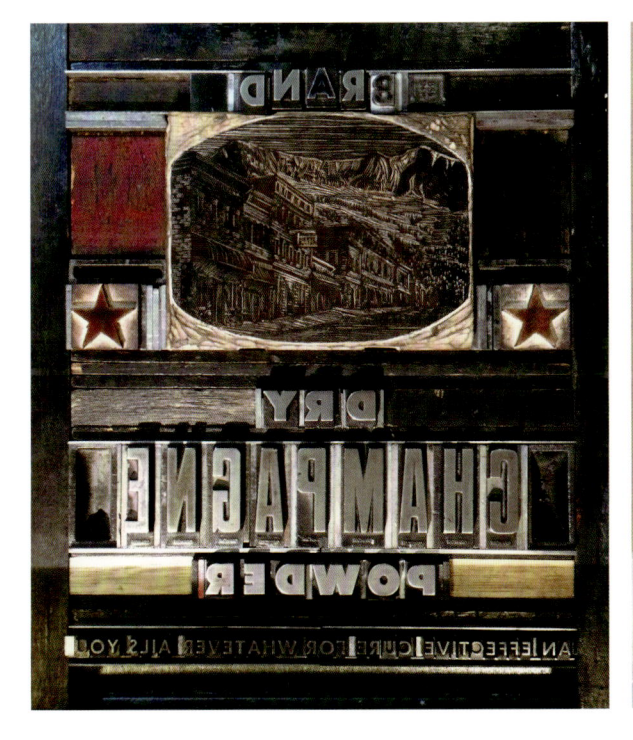

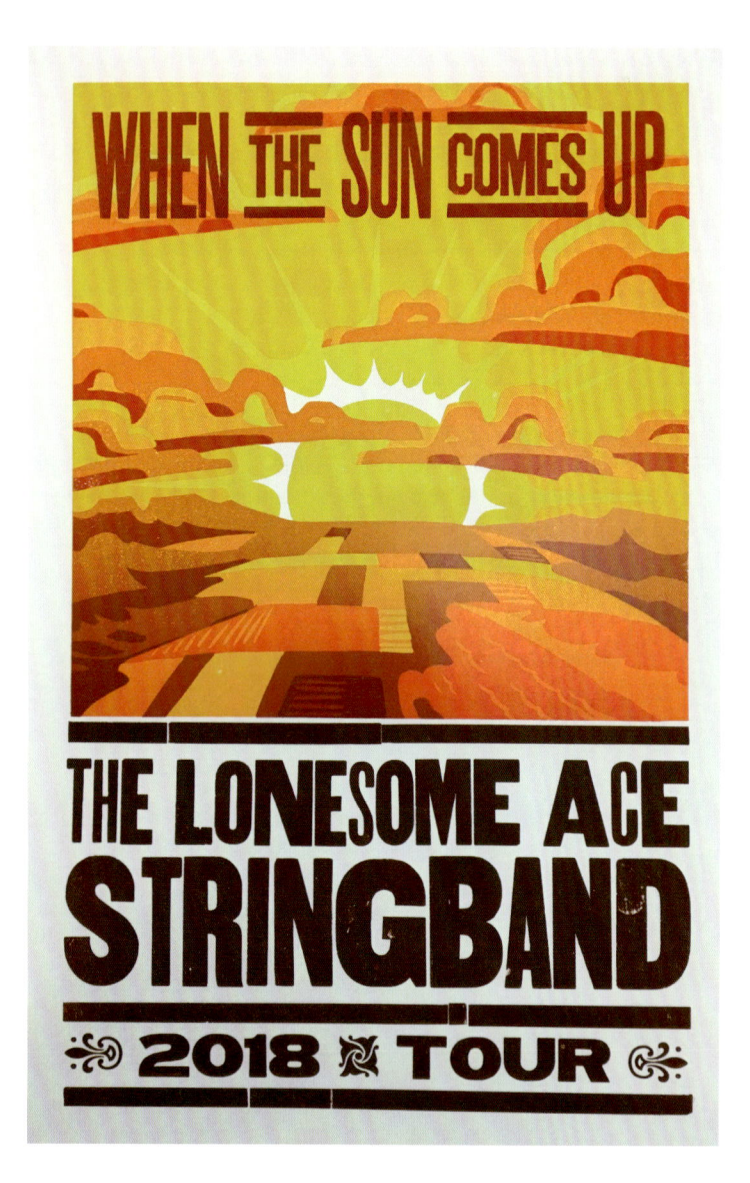

◄ The Lonesome Ace Stringband poster.
► Island Lake Lodge prints.

TAKE A HIKE
AT ISLAND LAKE LODGE

LET'S RIDE
AT ISLAND LAKE LODGE

GONE FISHING
ISLAND LAKE LODGE ~ FERNIE, BC

CAT SKIING
AT ISLAND LAKE LODGE

Get Impressed

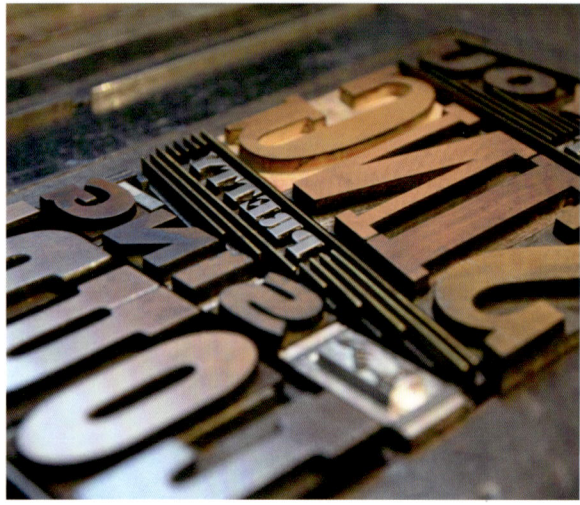

102

◀ Sing Pretty print.
▲ Bus print.

▲ Sarah Jane Scouten poster.

▶ One Lions gig poster.

▲ Elk River Spirits prints.

Get Impressed

**01 Clawhammer Press uses a variety of processes to get ink on paper. Could you share your usual process of designing and making?**

I normally start with a thumbnail sketch in pencil. This allows me to quickly imagine a layout, and revise it quickly. Once I've found a layout I like, I work up a more refined sketch that I use for approval from a client (if it's a commission) or as a guide to work on the finished product. I use this large sketch to transfer onto a linoleum block for a print, and the full-size transfer to pull and align any type that is incorporated into the composition. From there the print is hand-carved from wood or linoleum blocks and hand-printed layer by layer. The finished prints are left to set up, then trimmed and packed for sale or delivery.

**02 What will you take into consideration when working on different projects?**

The size, subject matter, and process vary quite a bit in my print shop. I enjoy the variety as it keeps me growing and evolving as an artist, and learning new techniques as a printer. These new ideas and processes allow my style to evolve as well, so the only qualification I have for taking on a project is that I get to use my hands. Over the years I've learned what I enjoy, and what I am good at, and what my equipment is set up for. I am happy to take a pass on work that falls outside those boundaries.

*Letterpress Factories, Initiatives, Museums, etc.*

**03  Your projects integrate hand-carved blocks, typography, and a slightly off-beat sense of humour. Why do you choose to work in this style? How do you balance these elements?**

I am passionate about typography as well as illustration. The challenge of combining those two loves has led me to a unique style that works well for communication pieces like music posters, album covers, and other projects where an image mixed with type is a requirement. Balancing these elements is different for every piece, each of which needs to have its own voice and tone. I look at a specific client or project and design something that fits their needs. I think about feel, layout, style, and type selection to blend the history of letterpress printing with a contemporary interpretation of the project.

**04  You have altered your artist and creative styles to match the limitations of a printing press. How do you break through the limitations? Could you tell us more about this?**

Printing on letterpress is all about being guided by the limitations. Many of these limits are physical and must be respected, so it's about finding a way to create something that fits within the boundaries but fulfills your vision. It is one of the aspects of letterpress that pushes my design thinking to new heights by challenging me to think about things in new ways when I reach a roadblock. As an example, I may picture using a large gothic font I have in my collection to print the word PIZZA, but very few large wood-type fonts have two "Zs" in them. Designing with letterpress means I may start with a "keystone" font and design outward from it. I might choose a font I know has two "Zs" and use that as the starting point. The result—as well as the process—will end up being quite different from digital design… for the better.

# INTERVIEW WITH CLAWHAMMER PRESS

# H.D.Y S.Y I.T F.Y?

How Do You See Yourself In Twenty Five Years?

Tipoteca 25

"What we like about letterpress is its high content of 'humanism', because it is made of the interaction between manual skills, creativity, and craftsmanship."

# TIPOTECA ITALIANA

**Cornuda, Italy**

Tipoteca Italiana is located in Cornuda, in a territory rich in art, history and culture. It connects historical memory and a creative approach, surrounded by a unique cultural, artistic and landscape context. Tipoteca honors the relationship between history and modernity. It is a little-known museum of type, fonts and print technology. The museum is home to printing machines from ancient times to more recent creations.

Tipoteca is a private, non-profit foundation created and promoted by the Antiga brothers, owners of the company Grafiche Antiga. Established in 1995, the foundation aims to give value to the Italian type and printing heritage. Tipoteca displays the work of type designers and printers, responsible for the aesthetics of books, magazines, and ephemera during a period full of artistic trends and social movements.

Since 2002, Tipoteca has been Italy's most comprehensive museum focusing on the history of type and graphic design, with collections from all over the country. Museum, archive, library, print shop, and auditorium… these are the dynamic, open, and working spaces where students, designers, and enthusiasts from all over the world can discover the history of type design and its protagonists. They can also learn more about the printing equipment, approach the creativity of design with vintage type and go further into printing culture and visual communication. As a mission, Tipoteca documents and promotes the history and the culture behind design and printing with letterpress. Designers from all over the world contribute to their training courses, educational activities and international workshops.

1-2. In Tipoteca, there are collections of historic printing machines from different eras.

Tipoteca offers high-quality printing using traditional methods. Vintage typography is perfect for printing private limited editions, visual identity printings, invitations for special events and openings, labels, announcements, posters and personal cards. There are casting and printing equipment, as well as a great collection of typefaces. "All the printing equipment and the typefaces were collected from Italian print shops. Most of them were closing because of the digital switch. We sent about 9,000 letters to all the print shops in the late 1990s, and more than 700 answered our request. For almost twenty years, the founder and president of Tipoteca, Mr. Silvio Antiga, visited several print shops and decided to save as much material as possible."

Tipoteca tries to share the interest and the importance of typographic culture. "Visitors aren't aware of how expressive typography can be. In the past, schools were teaching proper handwriting; nowadays, they should add a basic knowledge of typography since everyone is using fonts." Tipoteca also collaborates with publishing houses and artists to print projects using specific papers and inks suitable to letterpress printing. The strong and expressive quality of classic typography is the reason why most artists' books are now created with these beautiful letterforms.

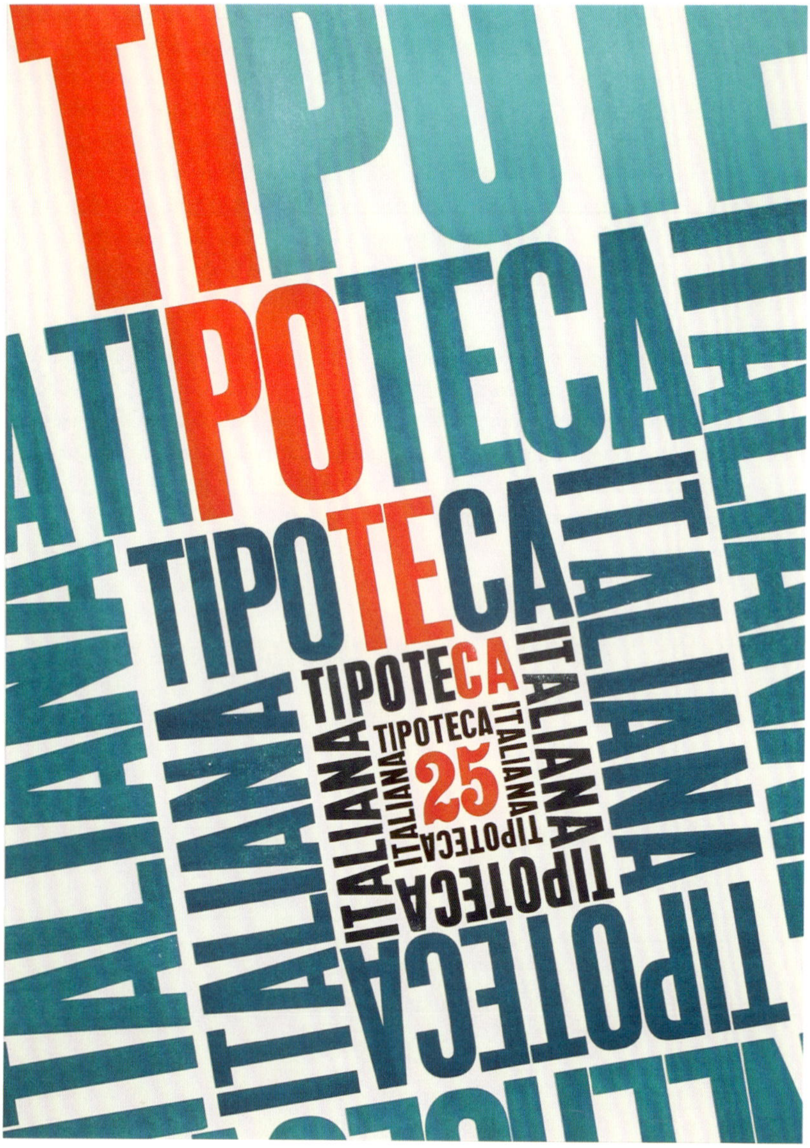
TIPOTECA
ITALIANA
TIPOTECA
ITALIANA
25

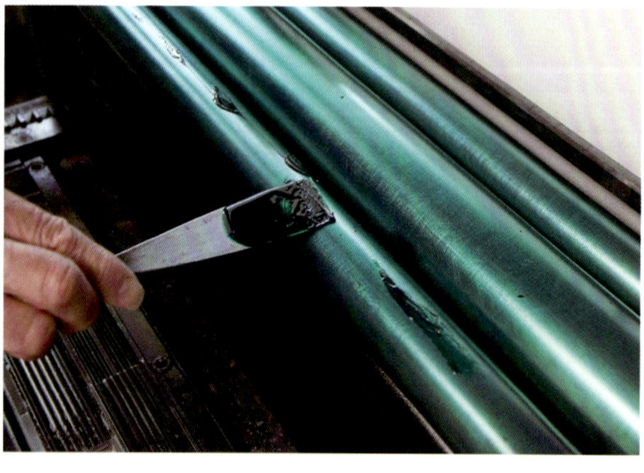

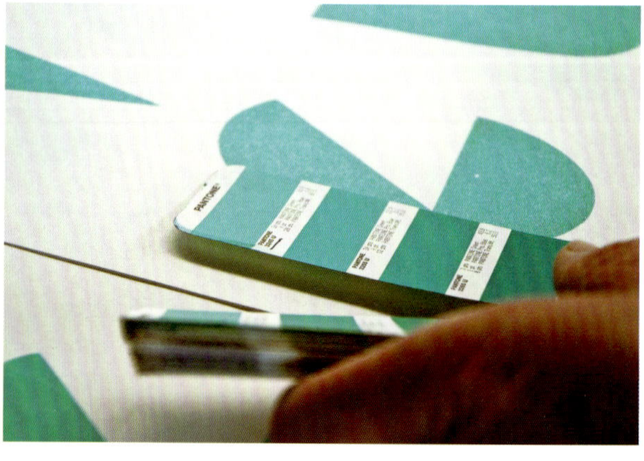

▲ Printing notebooks and calendars.

BENVENUTI
al più
GRANDIOSO
SPETTACOLO
DEL MONDO
GRANDE
LARGO
STRETTO
TONDO
ABBIAMO TIPI
DI TUTTI I TIPI
Tipoteca Italiana Fondazione
VIA CANAPIFICIO 3 31041 CORNUDA (TV)
tel.0039.0423.86338 WWW.TIPOTECA.IT

Letterpress Factories, Initiatives, Museums, etc.

◄► Printing items from posters to postcards.

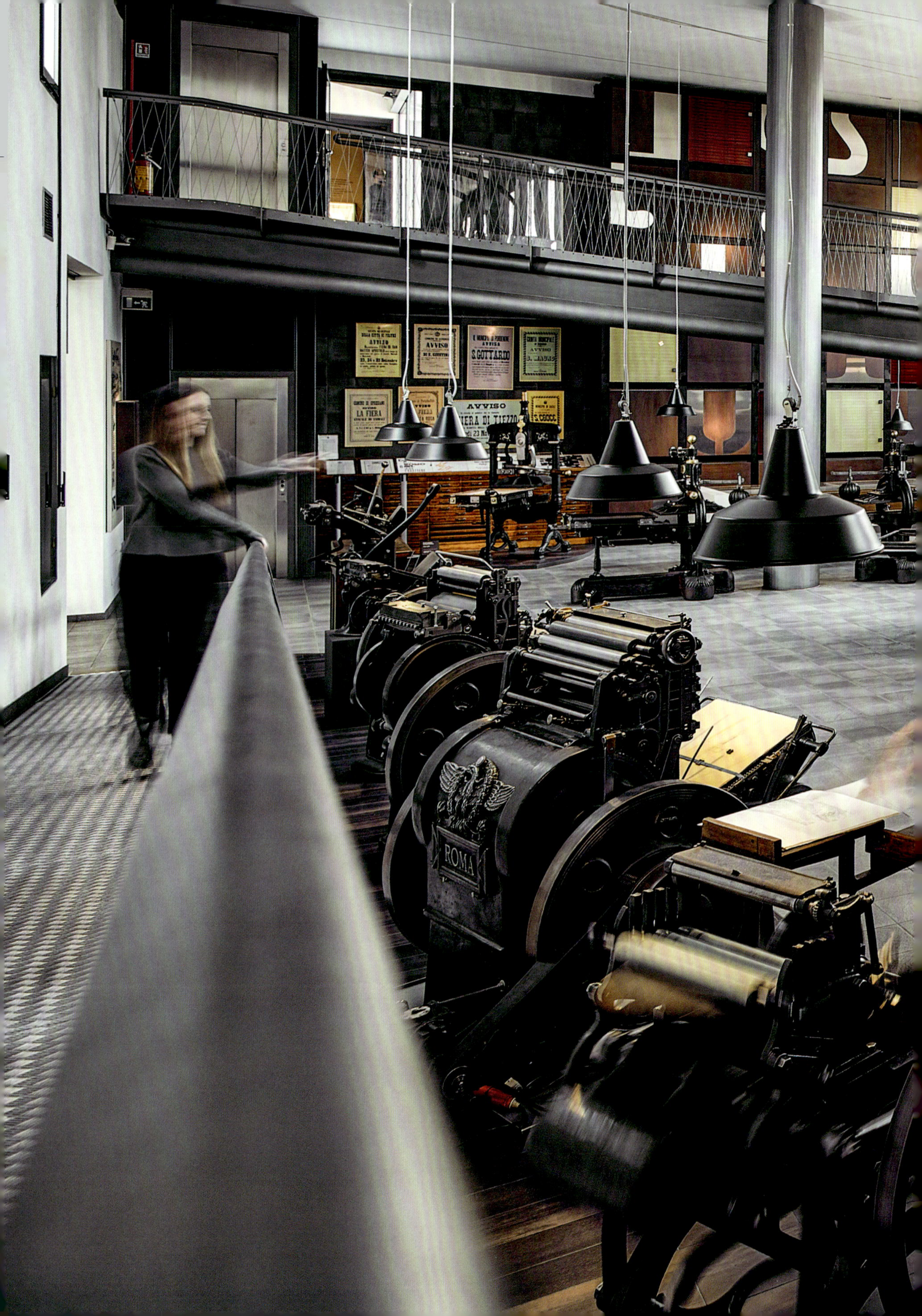
AVVISO
LA FIERA
ROMA

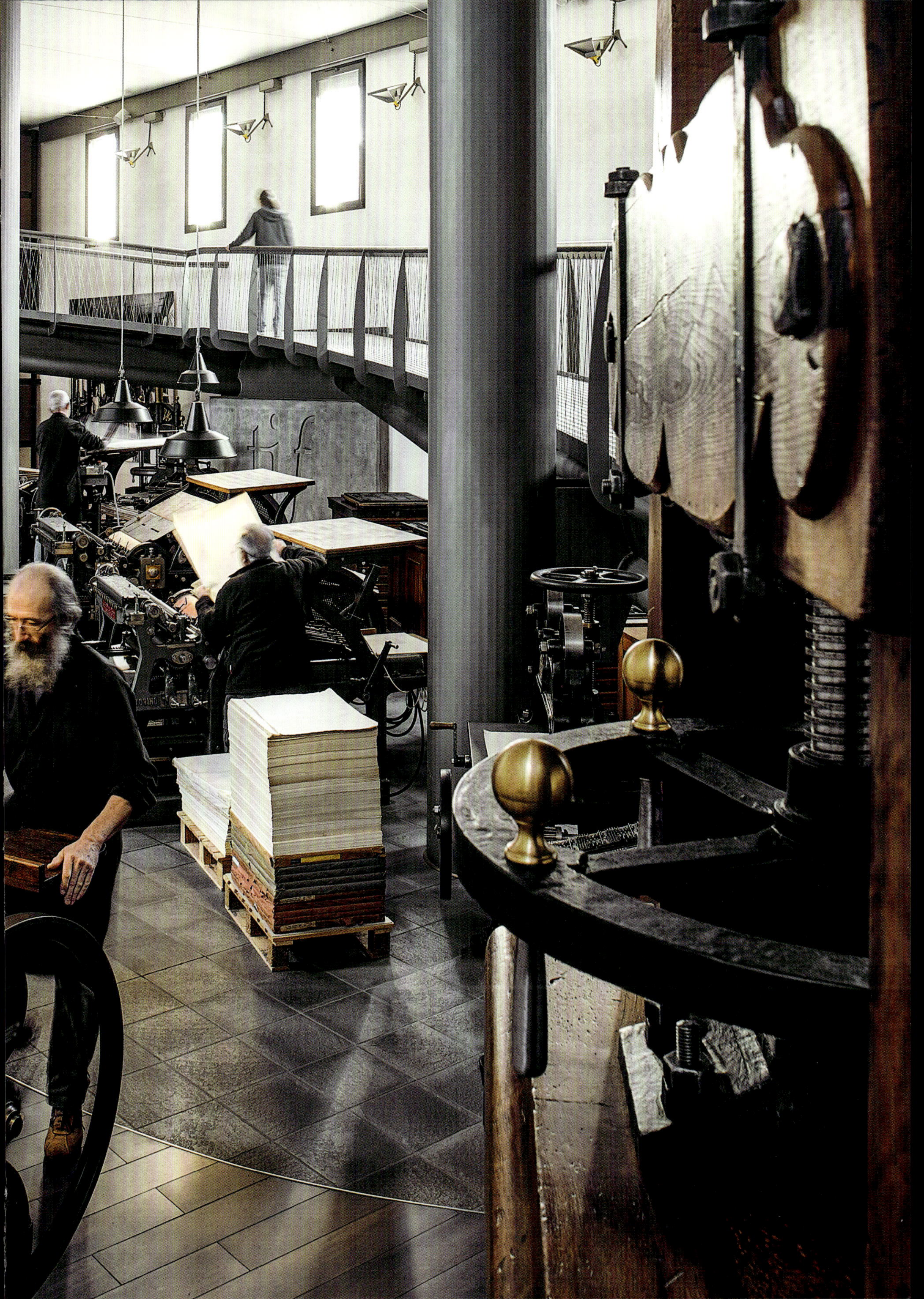

# INTERVIEW WITH

# TIPOTECA ITALIANA

***01** You have collected many typefaces from various regions. What are the differences between them?*

In Italy, most of the metal type was released by a few type foundries (Nebiolo, Reggiani, FTC, and a few others) so there aren't big differences among what we collected from the various regions. Probably the wood type collection shows more differences, because wood type "speaks" a more vernacular visual language, closer to people and local communities.

***02** Tipoteca encourages dialogue between past and present. What kind of dialogue do you think Tipoteca has with letterpress?*

Digital typography is everywhere: in our devices, on screens, in the urban landscape. The knowledge of our visual "roots" adds more interest and inspiration in contemporary design; that's why it's important to improve the history of type design and printing. When it comes to print on paper, letterpress adds a tangible feeling that speaks to all our senses. It adds quality and allure. A good printed card in letterpress is much more expressive and eloquent, especially because in general the public is flattened by the vision of graphics behind the screen. Letterpress has the grace to make graphics vibrant and pleasing, not only to the eyes.

***03** In what way do you discover and experience the beauty of letterpress?*

Like other designers, we share a passion and love for paper, ink, letterforms: Letterpress enhances this passion and gives power to printed communication. Somehow, it still preserves the role of the designer in all the steps of the process, and what we like about letterpress is its high content of "humanism", because it is made of the interaction between manual skills, creativity and craftsmanship.

Letterpress Factories, Initiatives, Museums, etc.

**04 Letterpress is now facing challenges in modern society. What do you think?**

We are aware of how much digital tools change our lives, habits and visions. We think that today contaminating techniques is probably the most interesting and challenging practice. So, as far as paper will be part of our world, for example, there will still be room for creativity and experimentation, craft, and art, also through letterpress. What's important is "exposing" young digital generations to these analog practices.

**05 Where do you think letterpress will evolve in the future?**

I can answer, quoting a very good friend, Erik Spiekermann: "Humans are analog. We only use digital tools." So, as far as humans will be around, the pleasure of touching and smelling inked paper should still be part of our mankind. Books and printed matter will become more and more "design objects" and not just a medium to share knowledge. Their physicality will still have a prominent place among people who love beauty.

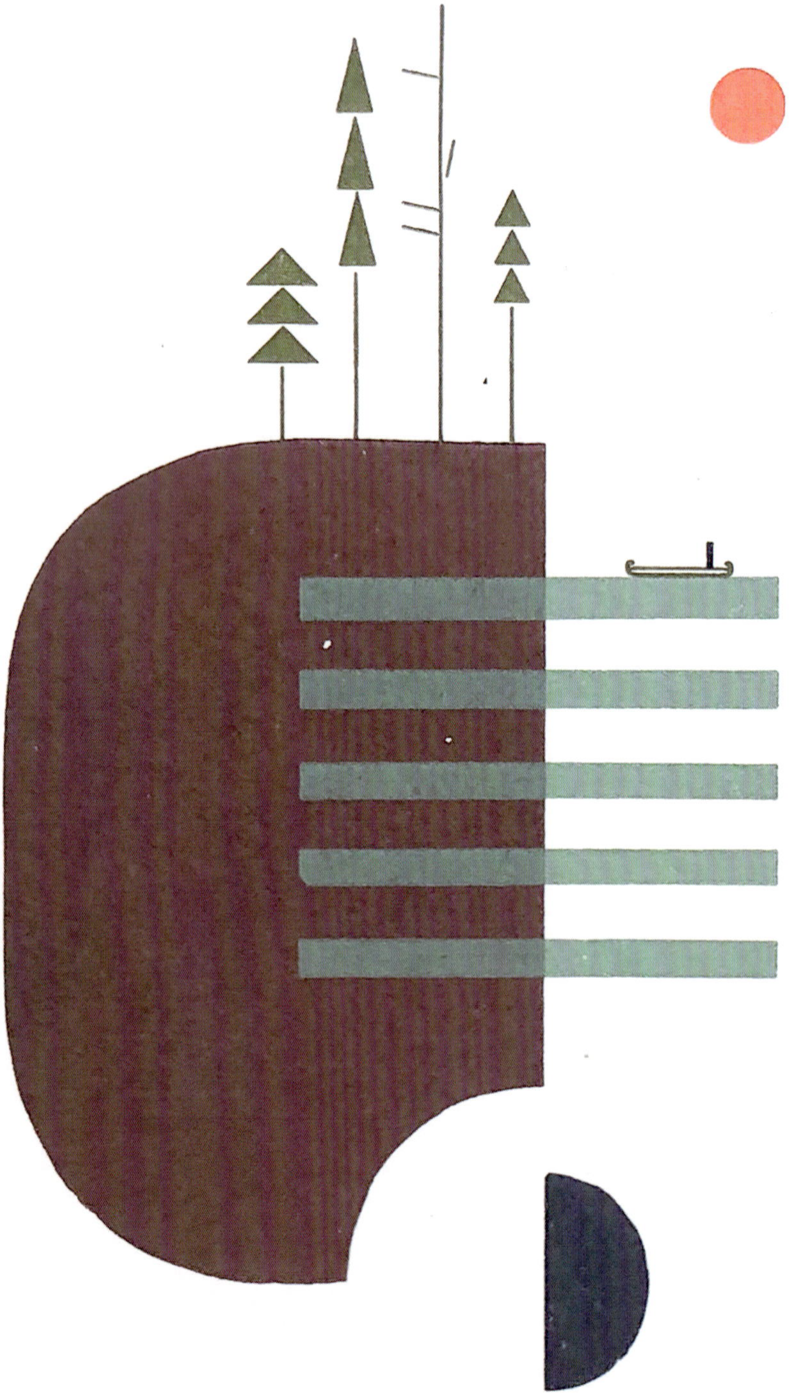

"As a grapheme-colour synesthete, I analyze the world through blocks of colour so I work to share that vibrant viewpoint with my audience by printing large hand-carved woodblocks alongside vintage type and ornaments."

# GINGERLY PRESS

**Pittsburgh, Pennsylvania, USA**

Gingerly Press is the printmaking studio practice of letterpress artist, Lindsay Schmittle. Lindsay discovered her love for old-school letterpress printing as a visual communications major at the University of Delaware. Jaded by the copious screen time and dull printing results of the digital design world, Lindsay found her sweet spot in the letterpress studio, at the intersection of design, illustration and hands-on craft.

After honing her skills at various print shops post-graduation, Lindsay began her own venture under the name of Gingerly Press. She relocated across the state of Pennsylvania to expand her studio practice in Pittsburgh in August 2019.

Inspired by her quiet time adventuring in the woods, Lindsay creates colourful, modern, and sustainable letterpress printed artworks and products with vintage type and hand-carved wood blocks. Her letterpress creations aim to inspire mindful connections with the natural world, one's communities, and one's mind and body. "I get a lot of my inspiration from my hiking and backpacking adventures. My printed interpretations of this inspiration come in two forms right now: floating semi-abstract landscapes with tiny trees, tents, canoes, and other adventuring 'characters' and minimalistic abstracts paired with a poetic line or story." In 2018, she printed a limited edition design series called *The Printed Walk: Georgia to Maine* about her thru-hike of The Appalachian Trail. She hopes these designs can conjure people's admiration for natural spaces and cultivate protection for preserving natural beauty around the world.

1. Photo by Porter Loves Photography.

2-3. Working tools.

Letterpress Factories, Initiatives, Museums, etc.

Also inspired by the historical power of the printing press to encourage social change, Lindsay aims to create a positive impact with every printed piece through her visual storytelling, bold wood type statements and raw materials used. Each Gingerly Press product is printed on 100% recycled paper and plants a native tree through a small business partnership with the National Forest Foundation.

▲ *Please Speak For The Trees And Vote* poster created for the Voter Mobilization Initiative led by The Amalgamated Colored Printers Association leading up to the 2020 USA election. Printed with metal ornaments and border rules as well as antique wood type.

Letterpress Factories, Initiatives, Museums, etc.

Photo by LeeAnn K. Photography.

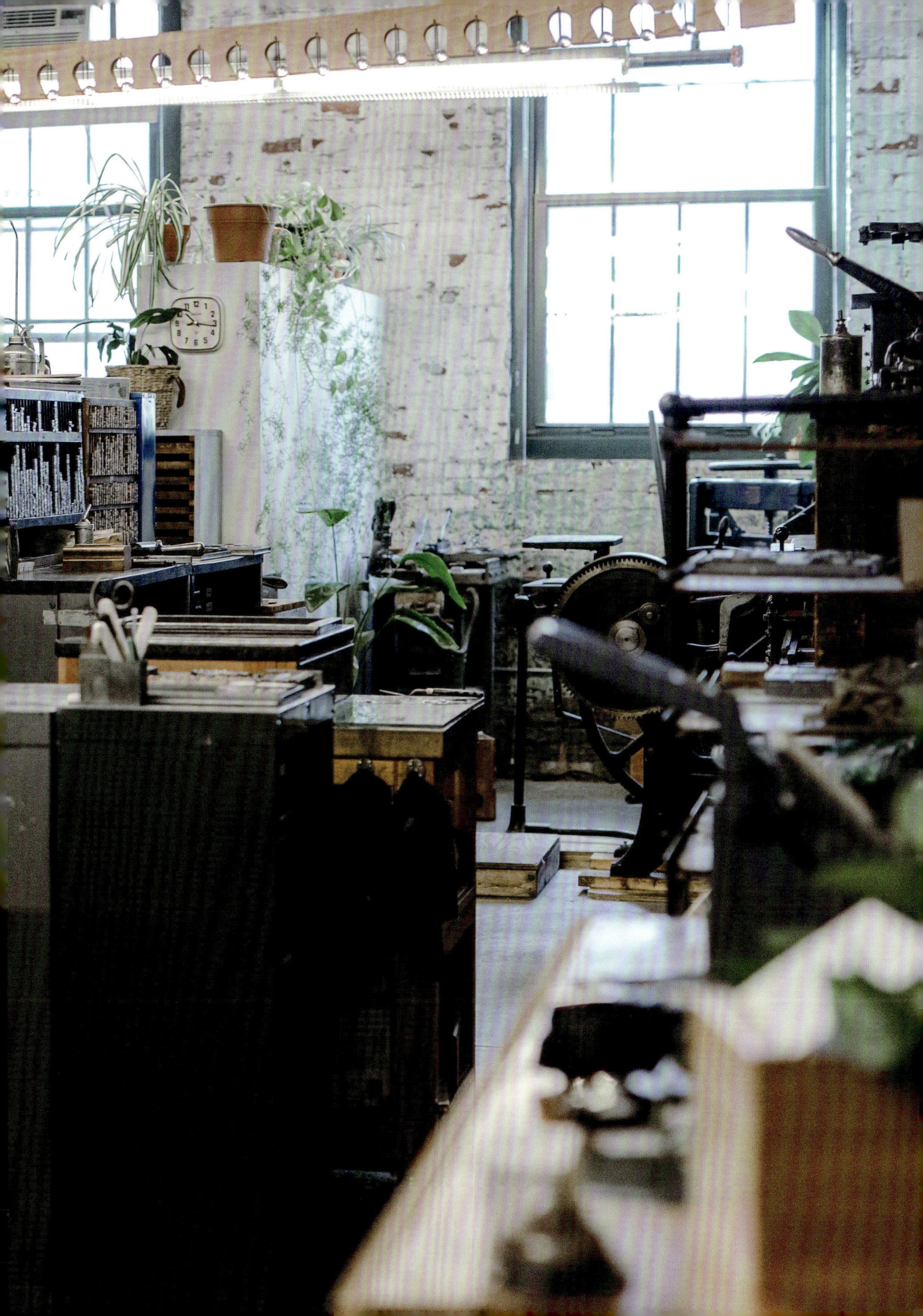

# INTERVIEW WITH GINGERLY PRESS

*01 Gingerly Press focuses on the old-time art of handset letterpress printing and modern design. Could you share your aesthetic?*

My colourful and modern graphic style certainly juxtaposes how it is made with the dusty old art of letterpress printing with vintage metal and wood type, but that's simply what I'm drawn to! As a grapheme-colour synesthete, I analyze the world through blocks of colour so I work to share that vibrant viewpoint with my audience by printing large hand-carved woodblocks. Often, to ground these woodblock prints as an abstract landscape, I use small geometric metal ornaments to print trees, tents, canoes and hammocks. I call these small grounding elements my "characters" in my abstracted landscapes because they provide a relatable sense of place in my compositions.

*02 You use a collection of metal and wood type. Where do you usually source them?*

I have collected my equipment from all over the place, but mostly it's all from older male printers who are retiring or have passed away. I have also won some equipment from letterpress-specific auction websites. It's funny because once you get into the field of handset letterpress, it feels like everyone is trying to hand off metal type or some dusty machine to you because they're excited to see someone young still working with the traditional techniques of printing with metal and wood type. I'm actually in the process of pairing down my type collection a bit so I have room one day for a larger Vandercook press for printing larger posters!

**03 What do you take into consideration when working on a letterpress work? Please share your working process.**

I have a handful of ways I initiate a new print, but most often, when beginning a letterpress print design, I am pulling a bunch of type and blocks from typecases and roughly arranging compositions on a scrap sheet of paper cut to the size of the finished piece. Then I proof print all of the type and blocks I might possibly use in the composition and scan those into the computer. On the computer, I'll mess with overlays and colour combinations until I arrive at a final composition I'm pleased with and I think my audience will like. I then reflect the design to wrong-reading and digitally print it to use as a to-scale guide for typesetting and carving any blocks I may be adding in. Sometimes design inspiration will spark from a simple journal sketch or a paper collage instead of directly from the type in my collection, but I still bring the design into the computer to test colour before proceeding to print in order to save valuable time and resources as a one-woman studio!

**04 Do you have any advice for those who want to pursue letterpress printing?**

My best advice for anyone who wants to pursue letterpress printing is to get involved with the international letterpress community. The community, which I call my letterpress family, has exceeded my expectations in supporting one another through sharing each other's work, providing opportunities to teach and travel, and assisting with acquiring and properly maintaining letterpress equipment—and they're just fun, like-minded, friendly people! Attend a Wayzgoose (printer's gathering/conference), take a workshop, or reach out to a printer you admire to get involved in the community!

Berlin
Berlin
Berlin
Berlin

Sonderausgabe
zur TypoBerlin
2018

Berlin

"I like the physical work, the slow process, and the lack of choices: not 100,000 fonts, not 10.7 million colours. The process is slow and you can see what you're doing in front of you,
not behind a screen."

# P98A

**Berlin, Germany**

p98a is an experimental letterpress workshop dedicated to letters, printing, and paper, founded in 2013 by Erik Spiekermann and housed in a historic building in Potsdamer Straße 98a, Berlin. They are a group of multi-disciplined designers, exploring how letterpress can be redefined in the 21st century through research, printing, collecting, publishing and making things. They work with metal and wood-type, several proof presses, a Boston Platen Press, and other traditional analog equipment. p98a combines these with digital technologies and uses all these techniques to produce a variety of products: posters, postcards, magazines and books. Objects like laser-cut key rings, upcycled notepads, letterpress gauges, and more all share a typographic theme. The studio also has a laser cutter, a router, a Ludlow caster, and a Risograph, but their superpower is polymer exposure.

p98a opines that the typeface has to suit the audience, the client, and the medium, which narrows the designer's options. Size is defined by the medium and the content. Designers have to consider everything: What is the page or screen size? How much text is there? Does it need to be read in a hurry or at leisure? Is it for short consultation only or continuous reading? How many hierarchies are there? How old is the audience? How much do they know about the topic? Do they want to read it or do they have to read it? Is the content technical or literary?

"Type for reading (not headlines or packaging) needs to be fairly conservative, but I like to use typefaces that have been designed recently, albeit within traditional constraints. For example, I just designed a book by a London author. The story is taking place in London, so I wanted to use Caslon font (Caslon worked in London),

1. p98a is founded by Erik Spiekermann.
2. p98a studio.

| 1. |   |
|----|---|
|    | 2.|

a traditional English type. I found a new version, called William, which is designed by a young Russian designer, Maria Doreuli. So a young designer gets exposure and the readers get a traditional typeface in a fresh version," Erik says.

At p98a, the artists run full-day workshops and studio tours. They welcome visitors to take part in a workshop. The artists will show the participants around the workshop, search for fonts, sketch their ideas, and finally print their own posters or cards. They offer help, advice and support.

Recalling how he found the joy of letterpress, Erik says, "I had a printing press when I was 12 but lost it in a fire in 1977. I then went back to letterpress printing after retirement from commercial design work in 2014. I like the physical work, the slow process, and the lack of choices: not 100,000 fonts, not 10.7 million colours. The process is slow and you can see what you're doing in front of you, not behind a screen."

Get Impressed

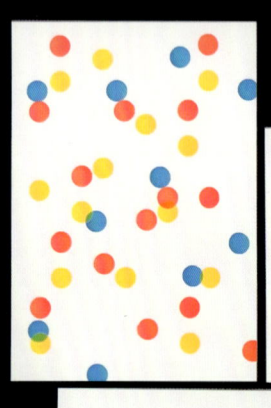

▲ p98a calendar.
◄ Positive project.
► Posters series.

**God is in the detalis.**

Ludwig Mies van der Rohe

**Better done than perfct**

**Be realistic, try the impossible.**

# INTERVIEW WITH

# P98A

**01 How does p98a redefine letterpress in the 21st century?**

We developed our own laser-setter to make polymer plates direct from data. Those plates are put onto a magnetic base in the Heidelberg Cylinder press from 1954. This way we get the advantage of digital typesetting with all its features and typographical choices (like modern versions of Caslon) and the deep black impression that only letterpress provides. Our motto is *Preservation through Production*. The only way to preserve the knowledge about using these old machines is to make things, unlike a museum where you cannot touch anything and will not really understand how things work.

**02 p98a continues to explore different printing technologies. What are the differences among them?**

They all have their advantages. The thing we like about letterpress printing is the 3-dimensional impression and the deep black it produces. We also like the slow process, as explained above and we know that this is not commercially viable for today. Its main purpose is to show how a page is built because there is no white space. A page composed of metal or wood type also needs the space between letters filled. It is like building a brick wall where the construction is visible and part of the aesthetic.

**03 Materials are important in your experiments. Why?**

Books and other printed objects serve more than one purpose: We read the content and we hold the object in our hands. Different papers, boards, and other materials feel different, look different, and smell different, appealing to more senses than our eyes.

Letterpress Factories, Initiatives, Museums, etc.

**04  p98a regularly sets up workshop sessions for a group of individuals or entire teams. What does p98a like to share with people?**

Digital designers have too many choices which can be a headache. In wood type, for example, we may only have two or three sizes and then only very few characters. That makes it easy to decide what to use and how to place letters; you have to use your skills to make it work. But you don't spend hours looking for more choices. Our most popular poster is "Better done than perfct". It happened because the type I had picked only had four lowercase "e" letters. Digital designers also like the fact that everything they do on the press is visible. No secret code, no backgrounds. We tell them that they have to clean up after work because letterpress is dirty work, and they even appreciate that because it means the work is really done. It is something you never quite know with a digital project.

**05  In what way does letterpress influence your life?**

It's what I do most of the time and it certainly is how I spent my retirement money. As that has almost run out, I am now looking for a sponsor to help run the workshop. It could be a digital publisher, a software company that wants something for its programmers to ground them, a large modern printing company that wants to preserve that heritage. After all, Germany is the country of Gutenberg where it all began in Europe.

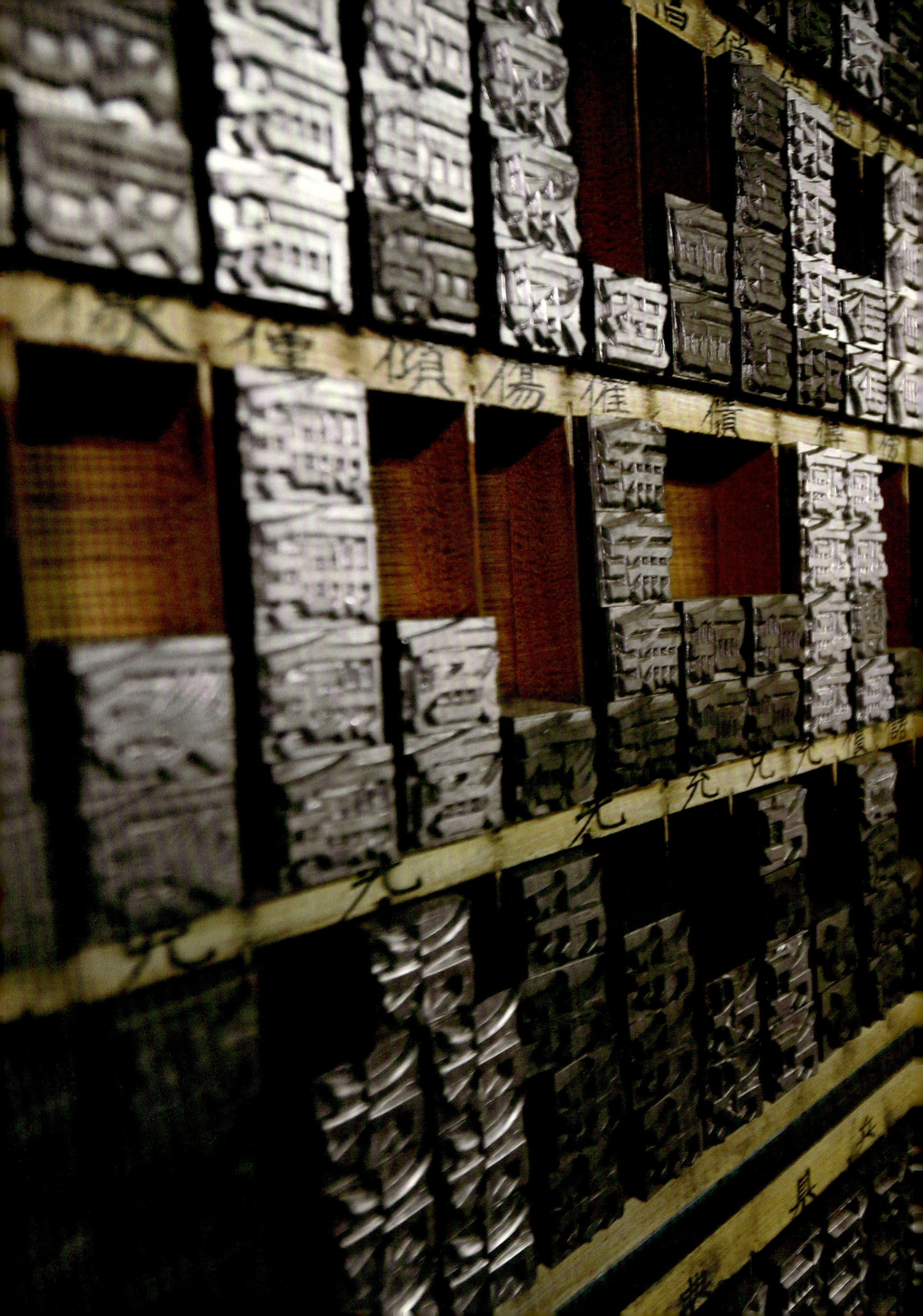

"We hope to inherit this technique and preserve the culture. This also depends on the joint efforts of the whole society to provide more resources and continue traditional industries. This is what we all expect."

# RI XING TYPE FOUNDRY

**Taiwan, China**

Get Impressed

Ri Xing Type Foundry was founded by Zhang Xiling in 1969. Now it is managed by his son, Zhang Jieguan. As the last type foundry in Taiwan, Ri Xing hopes to retain the technique of letterpress printing and to pass on the relevant knowledge and skills to traditional industry.

In the 1980s, letterpress printing was greatly challenged and hit by digitisation. Most of the letterpress shops closed permanently during that time. In 1988, Ri Xing introduced photoengraving and computerized typesetting into his business which helped his foundry to come through the crisis. That is a very important period for Ri Xing to become more popular with the public. It witnessed the movement of letterpress printing, from its prosperity to its near demise.

There are a large number of copper molds in Ri Xing Type Foundry. Repairing and mending are big tasks. Generally, the copper mold has a limited service life. It needs to receive a simple cleaning in order to maintain its normal usage. Once the mold is damaged, it cannot be repaired. Ri Xing has put a lot of effort into this. In order to make a new copper mold, Ri Xing typesets and scans the old type mold. By repairing and designing anew, they develop a new creation based on these font files. The foundry also produces digitised fonts for computer usage.

Zhang Jieguan intends to transform Ri Xing into a workshop that preserves the cultures of both the typecasting industry and letterpress printing. "The workshop is just one of the links in the letterpress printing industry chain. There are copper mold manufacturers on the top and printers below. The printer is responsible for

1-3. Zhang Jieguan is at work.

1.
2.
3.

140

typesetting, printing and binding. Ri Xing focuses solely on casting the ink type. The letterpress printing industry as mentioned has several sectors; each part has to be studied for a long time. For now, because Ri Xing is the last type foundry in Taiwan, it has the responsibility to preserve and sustain a complete picture of this traditional industry. That's why we hope to slowly transform it into a workshop—passing on the memory of every aspect to the new generation, showing them the beauty of this traditional industry and its cultural value," says Zhang.

Currently, Ri Xing looks forward to entering the education industry, training professionals and teaching students about this traditional craft. It also aims to build an educational system in colleges. Zhang is convinced that Ri Xing is limited if it works isolated outside the community. It has a long way to go. Zhang hopes that Ri Xing can be a standard for the whole world. People don't have to go to a museum to get close to letterpress printing. On the contrary, letterpress can be revived with increased access to the market.

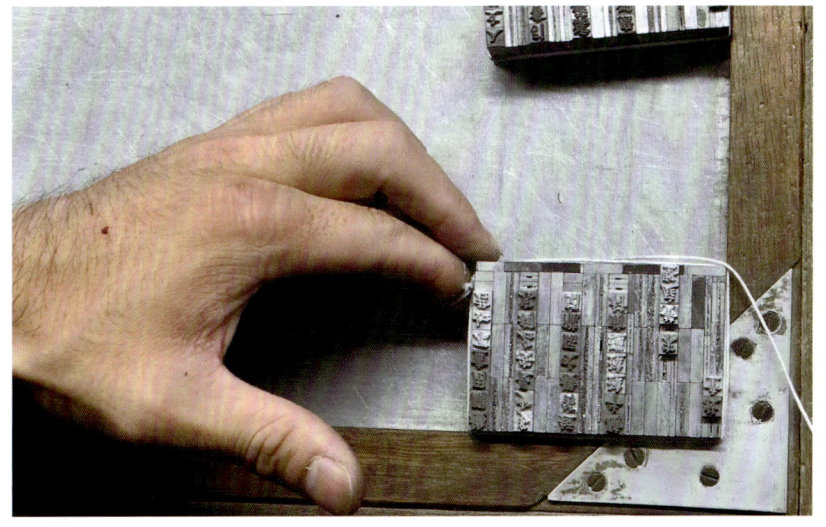

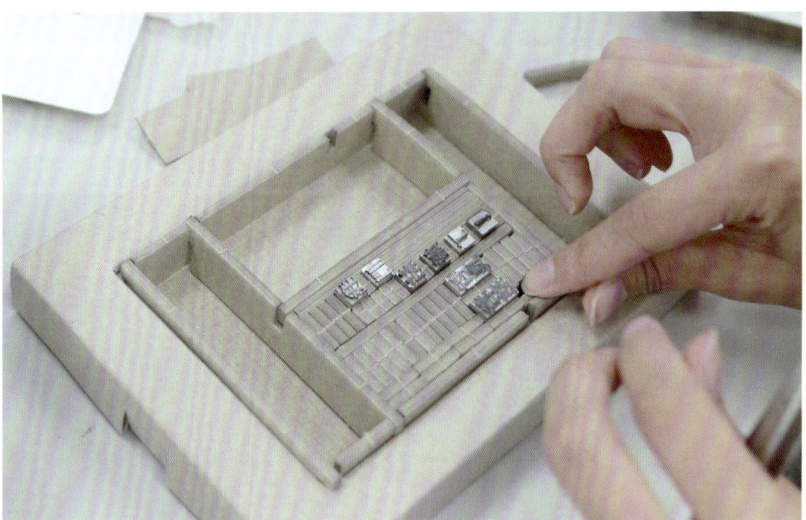

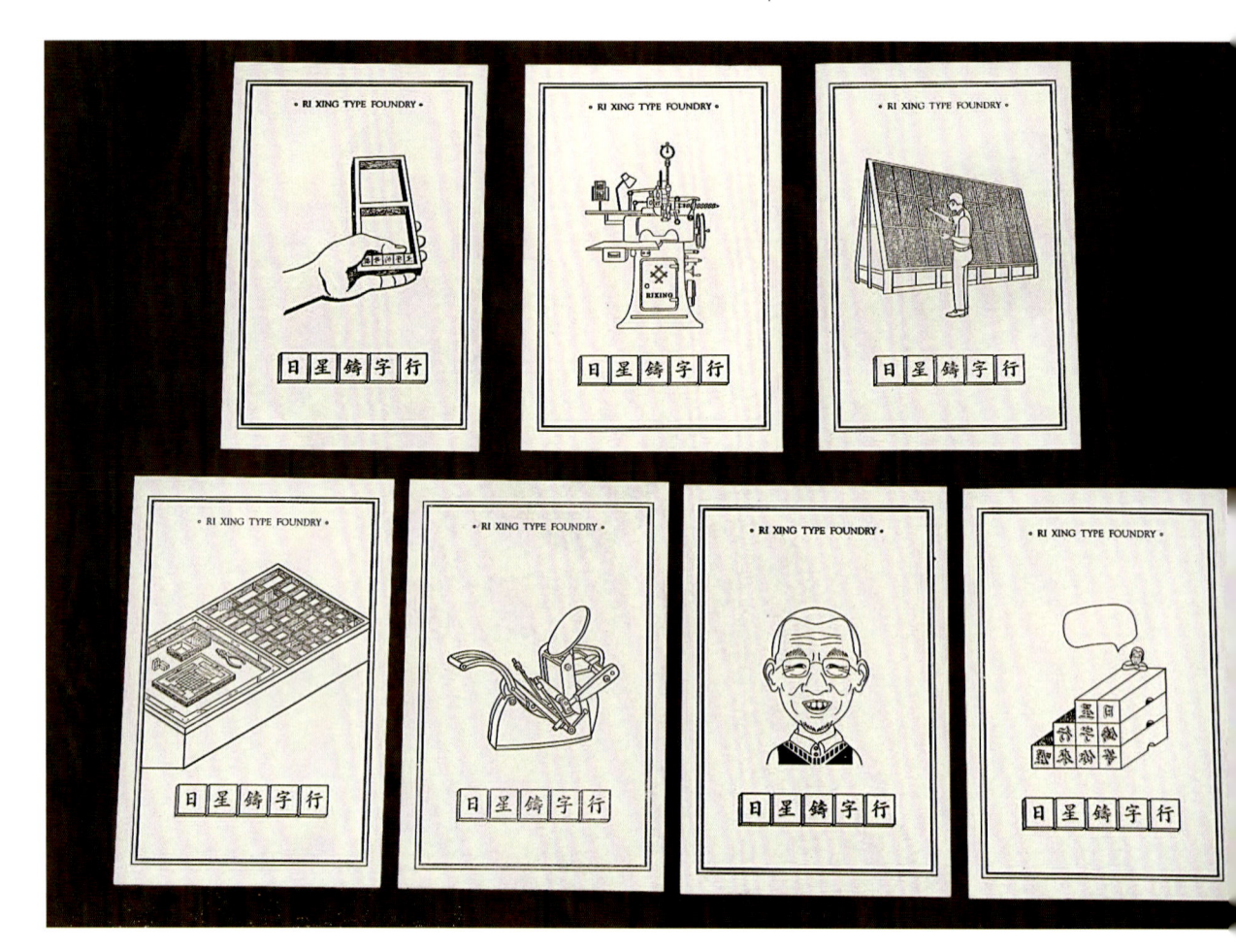

▲▶ Ri Xing Type Foundry also produces many letterpress products including cards, invitation, posters, etc.

Letterpress Factories, Initiatives, Museums, etc.

*01 What do you take into considerations with typesetting and layout design?*

The typesetting and layout design of letterpress printing is very important. These require years of experience accumulated by the masters. Once the master sees the manuscript, he has a very clear layout in mind. So generally speaking, the master does not need to think too much about it. It is a direct way of creating unless there are special requirements.

*02 What are your expectations for the future of letterpress printing?*

Strictly speaking, the letterpress printing industry has no advantage when competing with digital planographic printing, but it doesn't mean that it is useless. Although its cost is very high, the process is complicated; it takes a lot of labour and time to complete a printed object. There are different ways of printing: Ink type is a kind of letterpress printing; planographic printing is what we called colour printing; there are also intaglio printing and screen printing. Each type of printing has its own characteristics and beauty. Letterpress printing can still open up a certain market with its exquisite memory and uniqueness. It is something young people can continue applying in the future.

# INTERVIEW WITH RI XING TYPE FOUNDRY

**03  To ensure that historic culture can continue to be passed on, what kind of effort do we need to make?**

In fact, for the preservation of letterpress printing, the world has a common view that it will eventually be collected in museums or become an amateur hobby for a few enthusiasts. But for us, rather than being a traditional craft, letterpress printing is more important because of the Chinese characters we use. It has the most unique characters and special glyphs in the world. Letterpress printing nourishes our culture.

We hope to inherit this technique and preserve the culture. This also depends on the joint efforts of the whole society to provide more resources and continue traditional industries. This is what we all expect.

**04  Do you want to guide people to learn more about letterpress printing? Do you have any advice for them?**

Letterpress printing is a very special industry. For now, it has encountered quite a lot of problems. First of all, it's the machine. It is very difficult to get one, which will be the biggest obstacle for someone to enter this industry. Secondly, even if one were to acquire this technique, the market may not be sufficient enough to be viable economically. In the case of Ri Xing Type Foundry, we could provide 100,000 ink types per day. But in fact, the market may not need that much. So it's hard to cultivate a second type foundry. This is reality.

For those who want to learn letterpress printing, it will be easier in the future. As long as learners have access to machines, supplies, and expertise, they could gain a solid grasp of the techniques. But it is difficult to operate a type foundry because the market doesn't have the scale to allow them to do so. This is realistic and crucial.

They say that time can get away with what you actually have 2 change them yourself. Art is what you have 2 change. changes things but you

Andy Warhol

"It's an integral part of our lives, and it's everything we are. You can't separate letterpress printing from the printer. It has a transformative capacity, influencing the everyday but also functioning as an outlet for our feelings."

# THE SCHOOL OF BAD PRINTING

**USA/Argentina/The Netherlands**

The School of Bad Printing is founded by Amos Paul Kennedy Jr., Ro Barragán, and Jan-Willem. It is an international platform of believers in imperfection in print.

Amos Paul Kennedy Jr. is an American printer, book artist and papermaker best known for social and political commentary, particularly in printed posters. From an early age, Amos was interested in letters and books and studied calligraphy for several years. At the age of 40, he visited Colonial Williamsburg, a Virginia living history museum, and was mesmerized by an 18th-century print shop and book bindery demonstration. The incident so influenced him that he studied printing at a community-based letterpress shop in Chicago and, within a year, quit his AT&T systems analyst job, which he had held for nearly two decades, to continue his printmaking studies.

Ro Barragán earned her master's degree in Aesthetics and Art Theory from the National University of La Plata, Argentina. She has been developing artistic activities since 1994. Ro has participated in exhibitions, both collective and individual, in the modalities of painting, engraving, objects, digital art, installations and interactive art. She also develops art activities in the context of the street through posters. Ro teaches at the National University of La Plata's School of Fine Arts as well as manages Ilusión Gráfica, a graphic arts and letterpress printing workshop. Currently, she lives and works in the city of La Plata, Buenos Aires, Argentina.

Jan-Willem is a maximalist printer. His foundry Mizdruk is a studio that focuses on a misprint. "It's an error, a fault, a mistake, an inaccuracy, an omission, a slip, a blunder, or even a fallacy." Mizdruk doesn't see fault in the imperfect. On the contrary, differences and dissimilitudes fascinate Jan-Willem. "They create a new dynamic on

1-4. Inside Mizdruk's press studio.

paper, a human touch to the formalities of the mechanical in a world where industrial reproduction wants to smoothen anything and everything. I find comfort in the quirks of a misprint."

In the beginning, the trio just liked each other's posts online and never met in real life. Amos visited South America and met Ro Barragán first. Soon after, he visited Mizdruk in June, 2019. While printing together on Mizdruk's giant press, the idea of founding The School of Bad Printing was born. "We talked a lot about what kept us busy and how we all three seem to approach letterpress differently than most of our fellow printers—finding a common style in overlays," Jan-Willem recalls. He and Amos discovered that they were both fascinated by the work of the Dutch printer and early 20th-century artist Hendrik Werkman, who was one of the very first people to rebel against the printing status quo. At the time, his work was described as "bad printing". This is from where the name of The School of Bad Printing came.

"The idea was to have a platform of sorts for printers who like to print 'off-grid'—not as an institution but as a free and informal exchange network. Printers may join on the condition that they can make large sheets of paper dirty and meet some minor bad-printing requirements! We now have three main branches, but we're hoping it smudges across all continents. Since founding The School of Bad Printing, our talks have brought us closer together. We have discovered that we are a good trio with similar thoughts and actions, finding commonalities in our selfless need for sharing and exchanging ideas," says The School of Bad Printing.

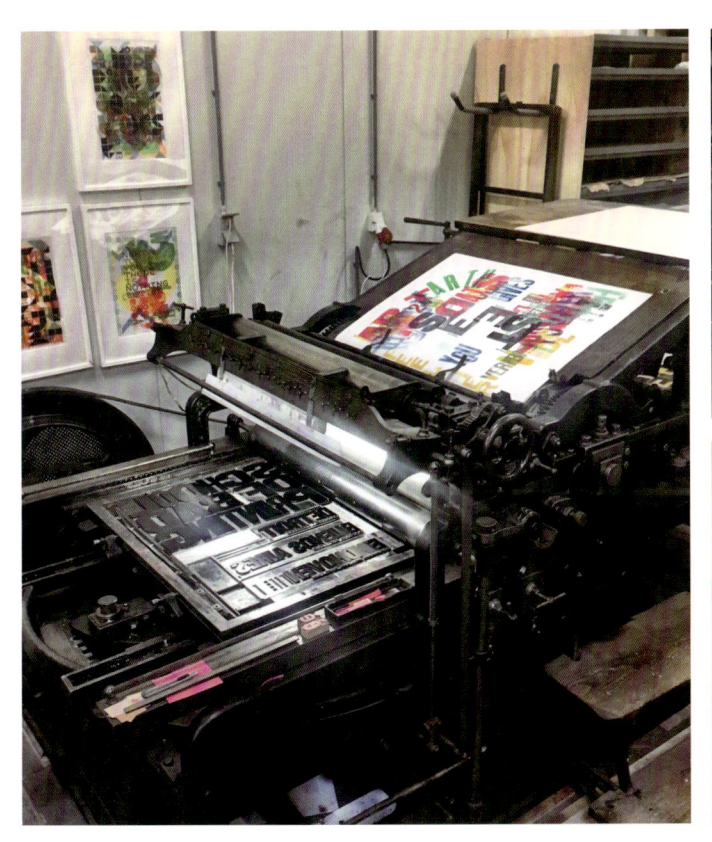

Get Impressed

Jan-Willem likes to mix alphabets, haphazardly, to form new design. His work is an imperfectly contemporary family of letters—sans and serif. He ventures with the unknown employing his mastery of tools and knowledge of materials ubiquitous from the past.

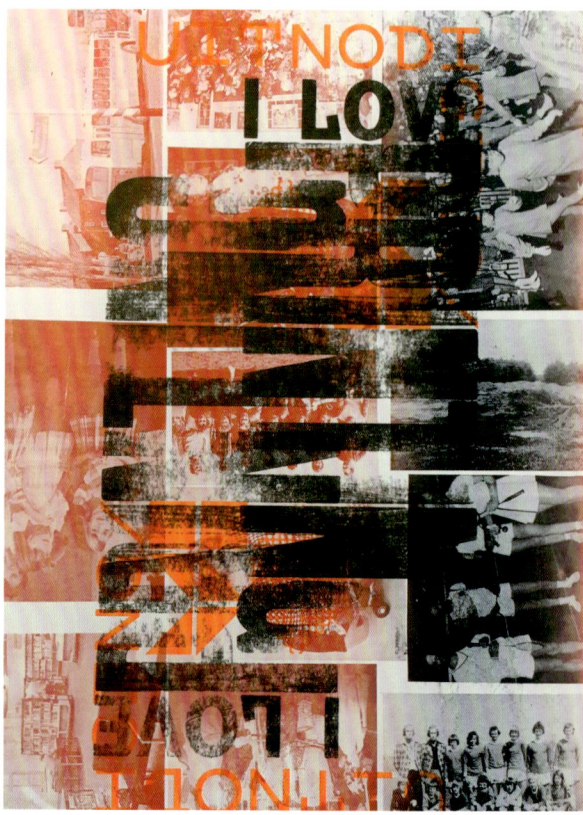

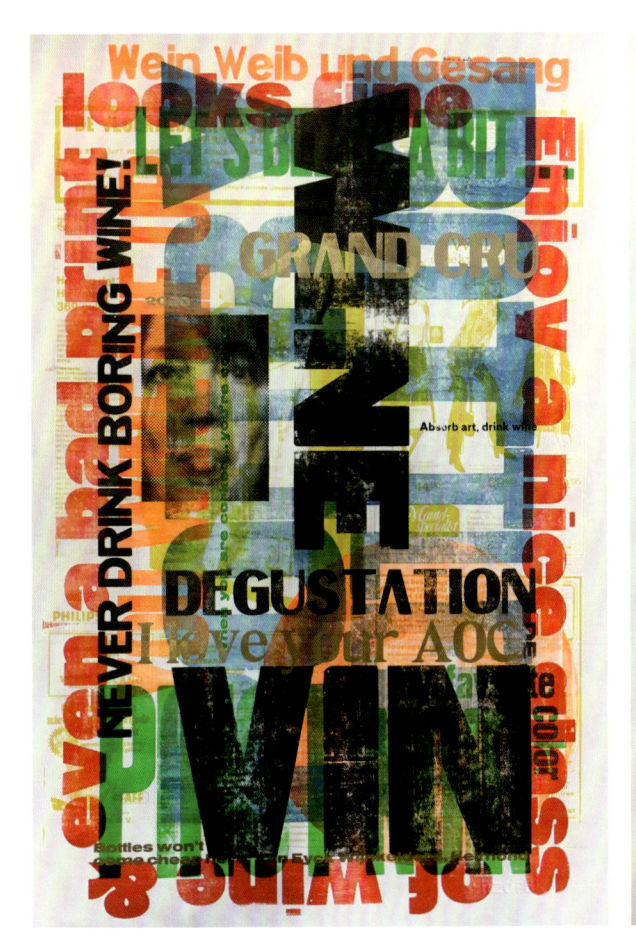

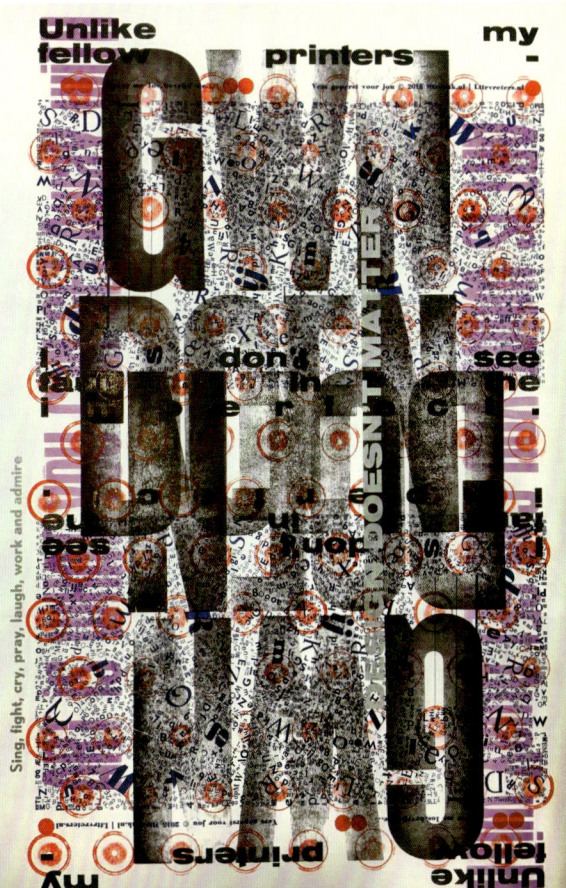

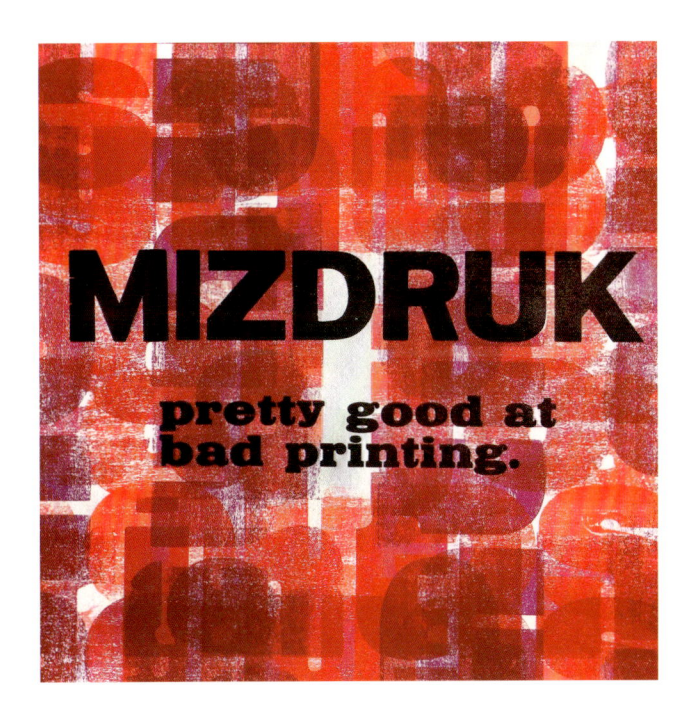

Letterpress Factories, Initiatives, Museums, etc.

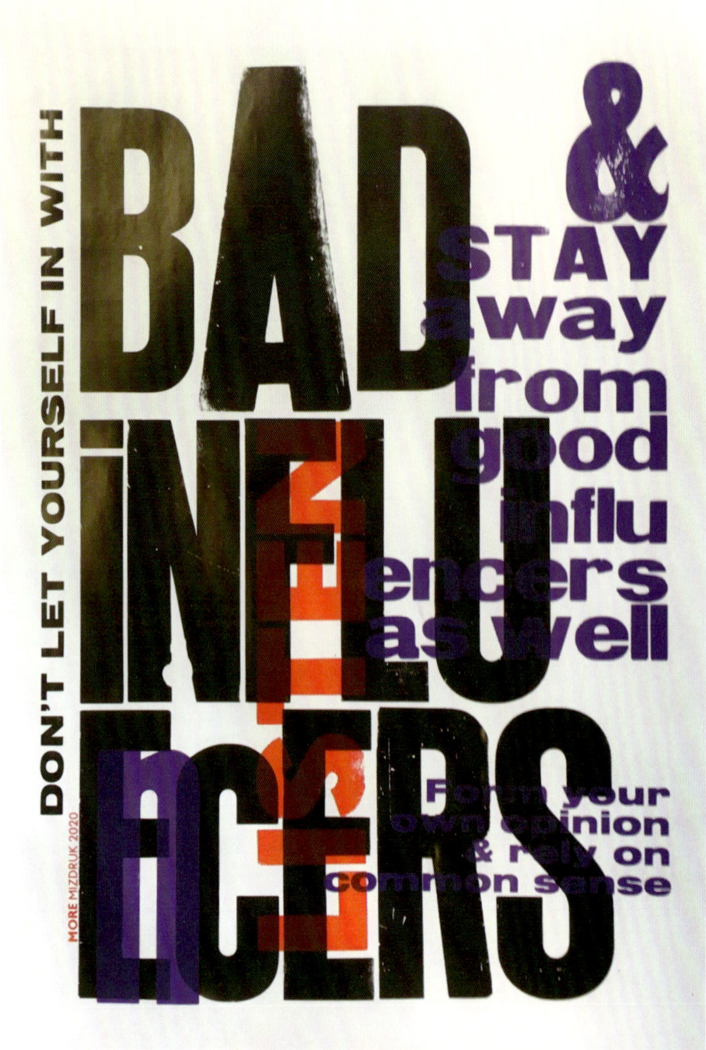
DON'T LET YOURSELF IN WITH
BAD
& STAY away from good influ encers as well
MORE MIZDRUK 2020

VO TE
VO TE

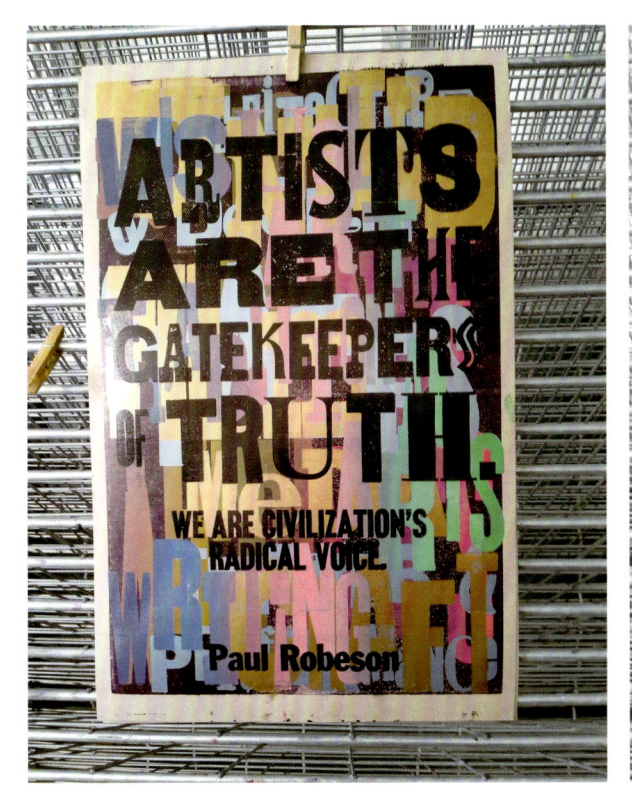

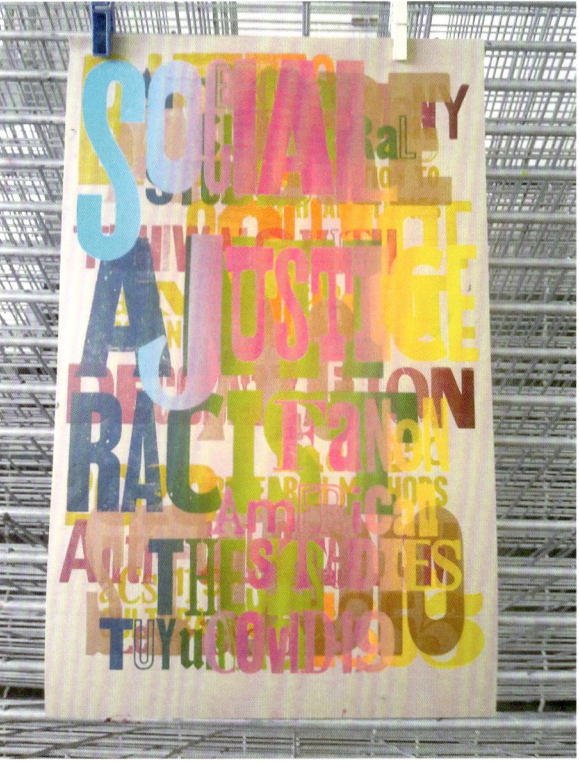

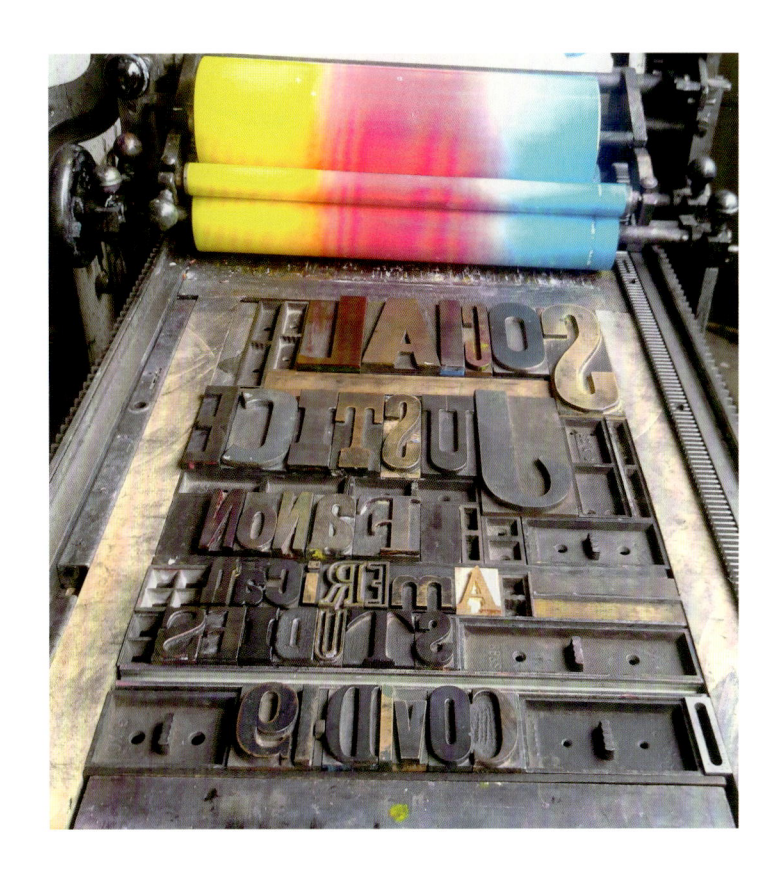

Letterpress Factories, Initiatives, Museums, etc.

▲ Amos Kennedy creates prints, posters and postcards from handset wood and metal type, oil-based inks, and eco-friendly and affordable chipboard.

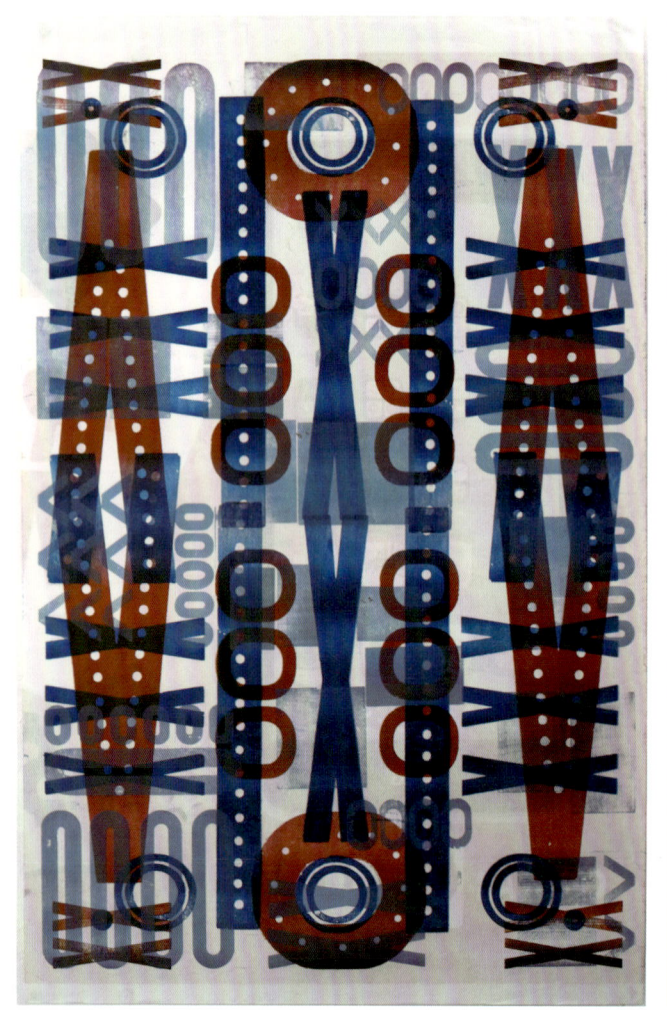

▲ Ro's typographic posters are printed with movable wooden letterpress in several superimposed layers. The work starts from the recycling of printing discarding posters, which were overprinted.

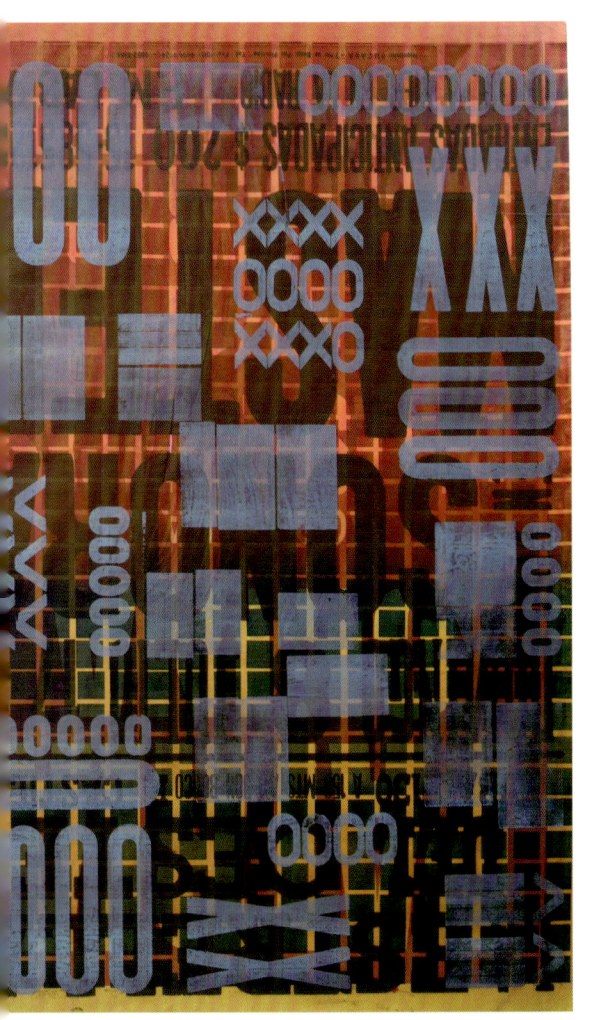

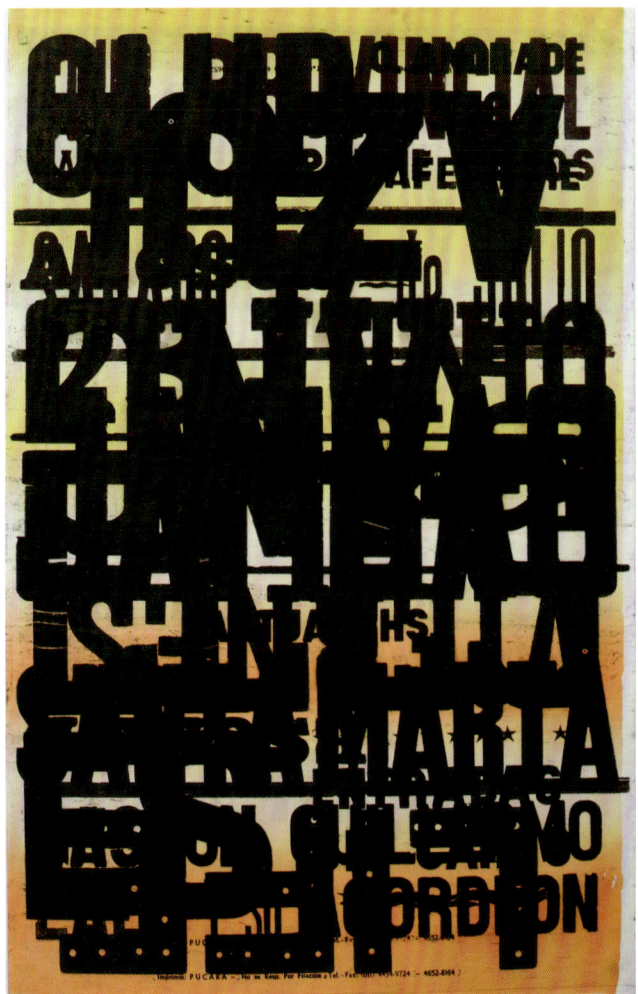

Letterpress Factories, Initiatives, Museums, etc.

# INTERVIEW WITH THE SCHOOL OF BAD PRINTING

**01 You all have different styles. What do you expect the viewer to receive from The School of Bad Printing?**

We are all individuals printing in our own unique style. Even if the styles are different, there is a common and relaxed way of working. It is all about self-expression, improvisation, diversity, and having a conversation. Why print a hundred identical copies when on the receiving end there are probably 100 different people? Printing should not be perfect but rather testify to both the process and the imprint of the printer's gesture. We are not here to make it immediately easy for the viewer to understand what's going on—we are The School of Bad Printing after all, and we cherish all letterpress deviations!

**02 A question to Jan-Willem: Imperfection runs through your works. What does imperfection mean to you?**

My fascination for imperfections in production has existed for a long time. Why do human beings want to surround themselves with perfect and smooth things while not being perfect themselves? In my former job, I used to see many commercial print shops. I would look in the bins near the presses at what was being discarded. These bins contained treasures! What was being thrown out because it was "wrong" (for whatever reason) was often much more appealing to me than the perfect ones on the print-pile. These "bad" prints carried an extra dimension: some sort of disobedience to the printer and graphic designer. Fortunately, letterpress is a craft in which many things can still be influenced during the printing process. So making changes for the better, or in my case worse, is not difficult.

**03 A question to Ro Barragán:** Words meet, split, overlap, blend, and juxtapose in your works. Why do you choose to work in this style? How do you balance these elements?

I speak in my work about communication and (in-)communication! I construct the poetics of the work through the superposition of legible texts and abstract forms, where messages are shown but also suggested and hidden. This results in a text-not-text that seeks to establish as strange what is well known: the word. I try to create a new possibility of language with elements of oral and written communication, which allows us to find new meaning from seemingly incomprehensible exploration. I look for balance through the poetics and aesthetics of each piece. As for colours, I have some favourites such as light blue, yellow, red and silver. With them, I form my basic palette, which I then vary every time. I also have favourite letters: "X", "O", "Z", "N", "E", "I". They allow me, thanks to their shape, to create and experiment with various patterns and textures. This is quite a usual process for me—using the alphabet as simple shapes regardless of their meaning, either by themselves or in the context of a word or phrase.

**04 A question to Amos Paul Kennedy Jr.:** Could you share with us your colour scheme?

I wouldn't make a point of a specific colour scheme. My palette is diverse. Also, I have never attempted to go against the letterpress but rather work within the limitations of the printing equipment, fully embracing each and every aspect that the process has to offer.

**05 Where do you always get inspired?**

I think our common inspiration is the "nonsense" of everyday life. Being alive is an inspiration! Triggers can be the environmental and social issues in society, but often it's the small things and moments in our daily lives that can be fantastic prompts. There is still so much that needs to be addressed, and only a limited quantity of time is available, so we never run out of ideas for what to print.

**06 In what way does letterpress influence your life?**

It's an integral part of our lives, and it's everything we are. You can't separate letterpress printing from the printer. It has a transformative capacity, influencing the everyday but also functioning as an outlet for our feelings. Arriving at the studio is a moment of happiness. You can share your knowledge with others or just research, study, experiment, and explore to your heart's content. What has become apparent though is that we might be artists more than we are proper printers.

Letterpress Factories, Initiatives, Museums, etc.

**07 How does The School of Bad Printing redefine letterpress in the 21st century?**

We established The SoBP as an exploratory and experimental mode of printing—shifting the letterpress from craft to a new form of art. We try to continue building on Werkman's legacy and free the text from the linear, homogeneous and rational system, establishing it as an expression where the poetics and aesthetic values merge and are enhanced. For us, letterpress printing is not only about defying the canon. It's an opportunity for exchange and friendship—building a community where it is possible to share intentions and desires whilst also thoroughly enjoying the process.

NOT

NOT

"Without letterpress, society, visual culture and life as we know it simply would not exist. And I firmly hold by that. The printing press and moveable type created the modern world as we know it."

# NORTH OR NOWT

**Leeds, UK**

1-3. A section of the North or Nowt studio and its working tools.

1.
2. 3.

Mike Ainsworth is the founder of North or Nowt. In the beginning, he moved from an industrial print job where he wasn't really allowed any creative input on prints, only technical input. Later, he started a day job as an instructor in printmaking at a university in Leeds in 2015, which made his founding of North or Nowt and discovery of the letterpress world happen simultaneously. He was allowed to be creative again and had enough time to develop and explore ideas and skills. "I'd never even had an opportunity to do letterpress, and I didn't have any knowledge of it at all when I started as an instructor. It was an area really underused by students, and staff weren't really interested in it at the time either," says Mike.

Mike read and taught himself and from there he has just kept getting more proficient and more invested in the process. With the help of other printers from around the UK and the world, he is really into this printing technique. Later, he founded North or Nowt.

North or Nowt is a Leeds-based printer in the UK, focused on designing and printing. First and foremost, North or Nowt has worked with screen print to create a lot of personal and client work. It started out specialising in gig poster printing, which is a bit of a niche field, but it's what Mike has always been drawn to and interested in. Through teaching print and printmaking in higher education institutions in Leeds, North or Nowt was introduced to letterpress and has over the last five years worked with and taken influence from the process.

Letterpress Factories, Initiatives, Museums, etc.

Talking about how letterpress influences life, Mike says, "I have this mini introduction that I always say to my students on their first letterpress class with me and to paraphrase it, that without letterpress, society, visual culture and life as we know it simply would not exist. And I firmly hold by that. The printing press and moveable type created the modern world as we know it."

North or Nowt gains inspiration from anything and everything. Mike keeps and collects anything that might be useful, which means his house and office are full of random books, magazines, adverts and catalogs. He also has hard drives filled with random folders of collections of images to work with at a later time. "With so much of my aesthetic relying on found imagery and resources, I can find interest and potentially useful materials wherever I look."

164

◀▶ North or Nowt had been asked to participate at Letterpress Workers (LPW) 2018, 2019 and 2020. LPW is an international event annually hosted in Milan, Italy where international letterpress printers and practitioners meet, discuss and print. Over the span of a week, allocated groups design and print a poster on a set theme, printing an edition large enough for all participants at LPW to retain a copy at the close of the event. These examples from LPW19 were based on the theme "Identity" and were North or Nowt's independent output, designed and printed over the space of three days revolving around the iconic movie phrase "I am Spartacus."

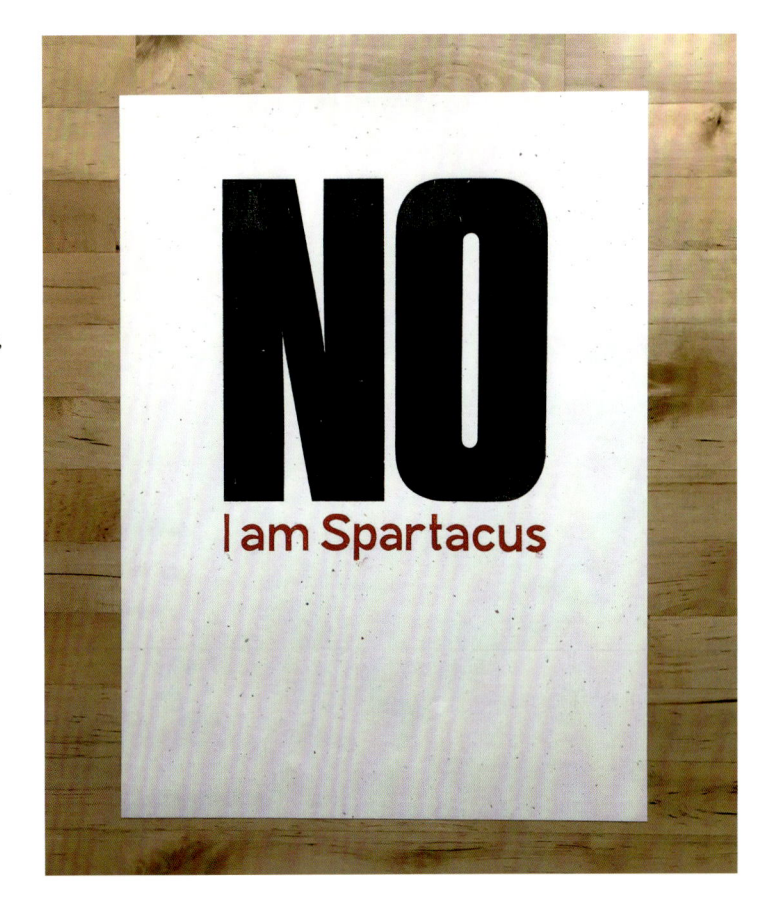

▲ North or Nowt has worked closely with Leeds-based restaurant OWT since their opening in 2018, creating branded merchandising and graphic design work in various forms using different printmaking methods. During OWT's relocation to the historic Corn Exchange of Leeds, North or Nowt was asked to create a range of merchandise, as well as a range of screen prints on paper and fabric. North or Nowt designed and printed a range of letterpress prints celebrating the restaurant and its excellent food, with an emphasis on their city's renowned grilled cheese sandwich.

**The Dog**

The dog, having understood every word,
didn't possess the vocabulary
or inclination to reply.

Luke Drozd     18 - 30     2020

▶ North or Nowt has collaborated with UK/Norway-based artist and illustrator Luke Drozd on multiple projects. One such project is the setting and printing of a selection of Drozd's short stories. These sometimes comical, sometimes dark but always very short stories have been set and printed using metal type to create limited editions.

# INTERVIEW WITH NORTH OR NOWT

**01 How do you describe the style of North or Nowt's print works? Could you share your aesthetic?**

I think some people would refer to us as "Punk" or "DIY" in our style and aesthetic. I don't really draw or paint so a lot of our work is made with found imagery and resources, manipulating them in various ways, so a lot of our work has a bit of a "cut and paste" style that is synonymous with Punk, DIY culture. And that's something I've always been drawn to through my love of music and going to gigs and seeing shows when I was younger and from seeing other amazing printers and designers like Print Mafia and John Yates when I was forming my style. Because we are so often using found imagery and resources, the visual style can often be drastically different between designs. For example, I could be making a design one week using vintage 1950s recipe instruction diagrams, and the next week I might be looking at hammer horror b-movie characters and posters. It really is all dictated by what or who the design is for.

**02 What does North or Nowt try to deliver through its letterpress works?**

I think because letterpress is such a time-consuming process, we will work with the process to deliver something that is considered and planned, something that has a purpose and goal. Unlike other print processes where I'll maybe use the print process to help me make decisions about a finalized piece of work, I wouldn't use letterpress in this way. Often for me, the decision to use letterpress is the culmination of our design process to realise our design intentions.

**03 North or Nowt has worked on many projects, which create merchandise for sale and art prints for exhibition and display. What will you take into consideration when working on various works?**

There is always a huge difference between working on a project for yourself and working on something for a client. When I'm working for myself, I am constantly asking, "Is this actually any good," or "Do I actually like this?" Very rarely do I consider "would someone buy this" which I probably should do a little bit more of. Most of the time with personal projects, it's an idea that has been stuck in my head for a while that I simply need to get out of me and see if it works, just to make space for new ideas. And I think that's a really useful way to work for clients too. All ideas, even the ridiculous ones, are useful for me just to get my mind working. It's not that there are no bad ideas (there definitely are bad ones…) but everything you do before you get to the final design or concept that satisfies yourself and the client is all part of the process of getting to that point.

**04 What do you think of the future of letterpress printing, especially in this digital era?**

This question keeps coming up whenever we talk about letterpress in the 21st century, and to paraphrase Carl Middleton (UK), letterpress is a time heavy process that is limited by access to materials and equipment that are becoming increasingly scarce and expensive and in a time where digital innovation and development happens seemingly on a daily basis. But we are still printing with letterpress, we are still talking about letterpress, there are clients who still want letterpress. If anything, the digital era has benefited the letterpress world rather than impeded it.

As practitioners, we are more connected and aware of one another than ever, again to paraphrase Carl Middleton, creating a "letterpress fraternity", where skills and knowledge are shared across generations and international borders, imparting skills and knowledge as well as innovative new ideas and developments. We have access to new materials allowing for the next developmental stage of letterpress, with 3D printing, laser cutting, and CNC (computer numerical control) routing becoming increasingly important pieces of equipment and skills for those interested in a future in letterpress.

# 05

**More Letterpress Projects...**

## Infinitive Factory

The Infinitive Factory stands for high-quality custom-made letterpress. The company is known for pushing limits in the field of letterpress and experimenting with new ways of creating overwhelming effects for their clients. Studio Bruch drew inspiration from creating and arranging the printing plates and decided to use the suitable skeleton of the letters "I" and "F" to create a fine structure that serves as the basis of a highly flexible branding system that can be adapted to every proportion. The simple and clear composition also functions as a flexible frame for graphics, illustrations and typography to show the countless possibilities of printing and finishing with letterpress printing machines.

Design Agency: **Studio Bruch** / Creative Direction: **Studio Bruch** / Art Direction: **Studio Bruch** / Illustration: **Studio Bruch, Elke Bauer** / Letterpress: **Infinitive Factory**

More Letterpress Projects...

## If Earth Is Our Mother—Coffee Grounds Candles

The inspiration for If Earth Is Our Mother derived from the traditional Hawaiian therapy of Ho'oponopono and is comprised of four phases of cleansing and healing: "I love you", "I am sorry", "Please forgive me" and "Thank you". It is intended to build a connection between humans and the earth. While using a pen to write out the phrases of Ho'oponopono on the label of the bottle, mother earth begins to repair relationships from the heart. If Earth Is Our Mother is a perspective of our planet. The designer used small dots to form the land. The dots represent candle lights and give off the idea that there are countless people holding up a candle all over the world on Earth Day.

Design Agency: **Hillz Design** / Art Direction: **Hio Cheng Choi** / Design: **Hio Cheng Choi** / Clients: **Starbucks, ÄiÄi Illum Lab** / Photography: **Junyou Liu**

More Letterpress Projects...

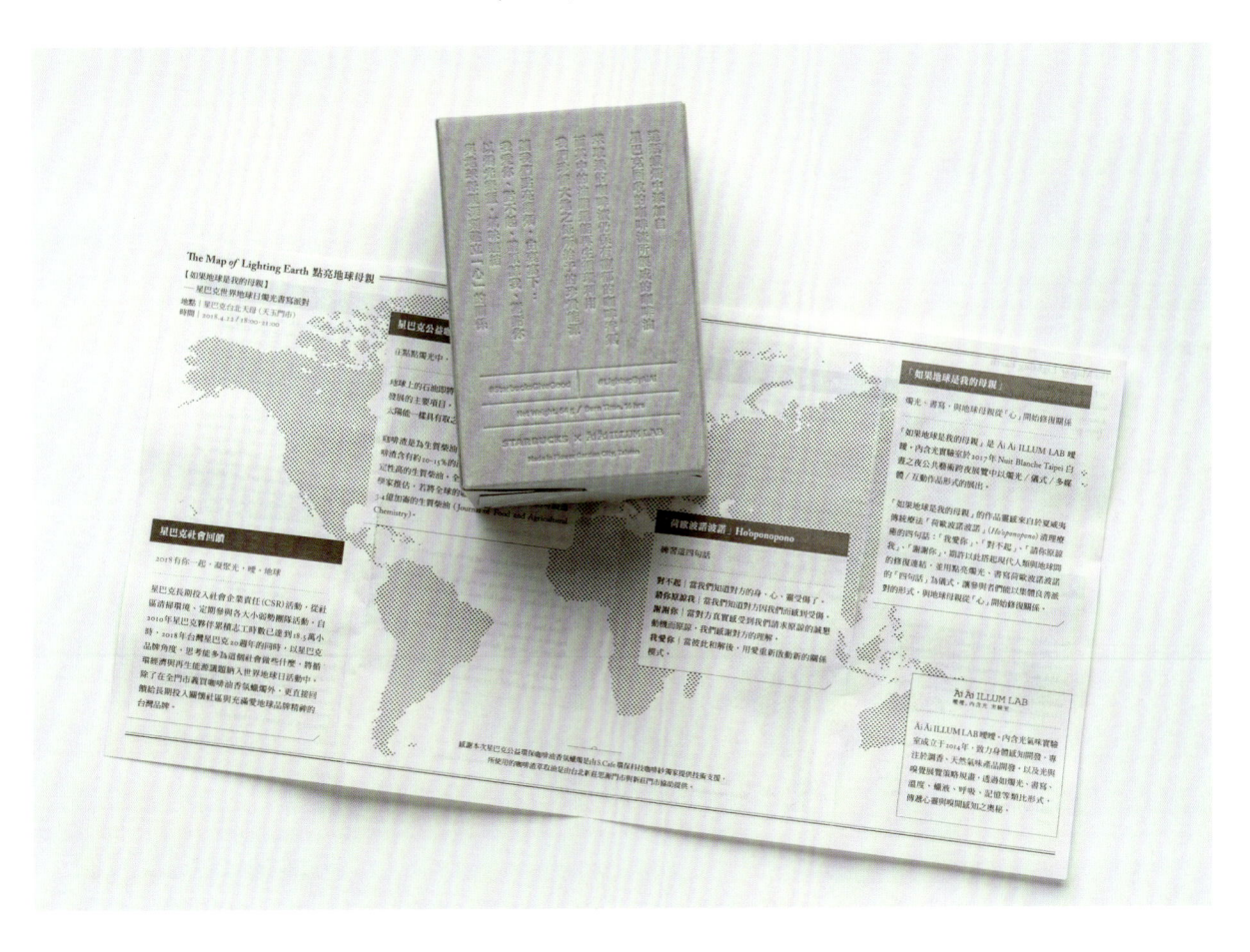

## Wedding Pass Set

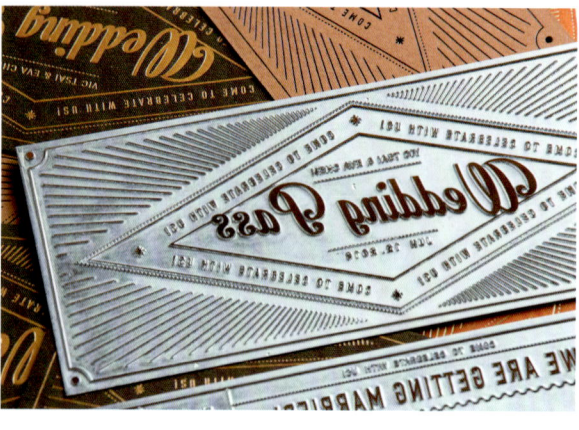

Wedding Pass Set is a wedding invitation card designed for Vic and Eva. With the high-quality, beautiful texture, and complicated printing processes, the card shows sincerity and gives an impressive experience. Furthermore, for different ages of invitees, designers utilised four different colour sets. The main card is designed as a ticket, and the small card is designed as a bookmark. They hope this card can be an art collection after the wedding.

Design Agency: **StudioPros** / Design: **Yi-Hsuan Li** /
Printing: **Wei-Yang Printing Enterprise Co., Ltd** / Clients: **Vic Tsai, Eva Chen** /
Photography: **Shengyuan Hsu**

More Letterpress Projects...

## The 2019 Letterpress Calendar

The deluxe edition front cover is on gold paper, with gold hot foil and black hot foil. All the pages are in gold hot foil on black paper. The standard edition front cover is on black paper with gold and black hot foil. The pages are letterpress printed in black on white and light grey pure cotton paper.

The cover is designed by Mr Cup. This year's edition features unique designs by Nick Misani, Ginger Monkey (AKA, Tom Lane), Dan Grett, Peter Voth, Kelsy Stromski, Christian Watson of 1924.us, Tuyet Duyet, Reno Orange, Dan Gretta and Nancy Rouemy.

Design: **Mr Cup**

NEVER
LET
SMALL
MINDS
CONVINCE
YOU
THAT your DREAMS
ARE TOO
BIG
MARCH
03 2019
RUE NATIONALE
CASTELNAUDARY

WHAT YOU'VE ALWAYS DONE
WHAT YOU'VE ALWAYS GOTTEN
FEBRUARY
02 2019
CH. BURMEISTER
RUE NATIONALE
CASTELNAUDARY
MR-CUP.COM
PRESENTS

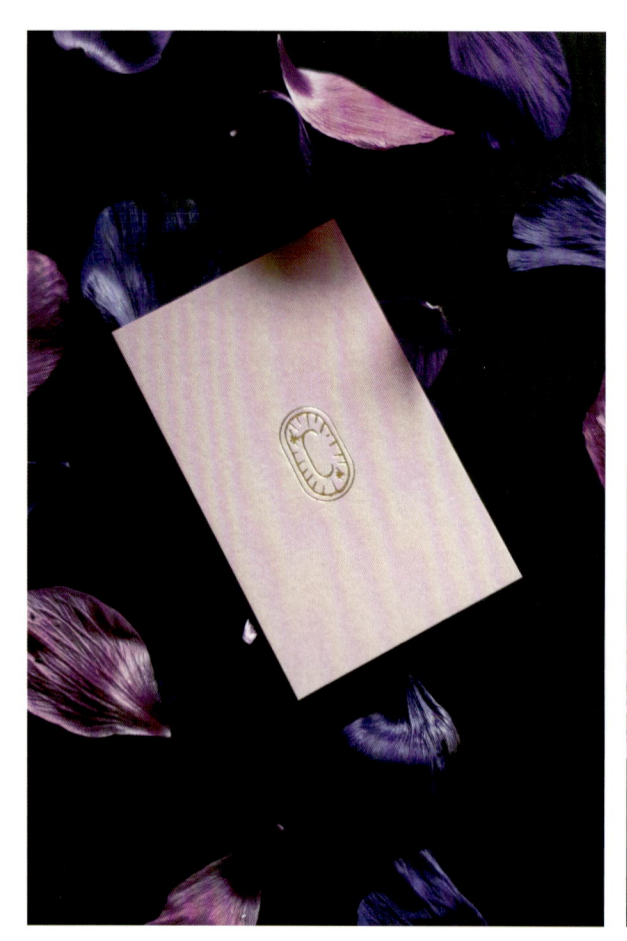

**Chalvin Paris**

This is a brand identity designed for a Paris-based agency.

Design: **Alexia ROUX**

More Letterpress Projects...

### Muchacha

Muchacha is a French restaurant and bar operated with a Latin American theme. This project is designed for its brand identity.

Design: **Alexia ROUX**

Get Impressed

## Happy White Year

This project is a promotional calendar to congratulate the New Year to customers and Minke, a creative provider of graphic services. In a frigid landscape, the native people of the far north are able to distinguish 30 shades of white. In Minke's warmer world, designers have found at least 12 shades. If every year has a colour, 2015 looks to be a shade of white, like a blank page offering a space on which to act, to write. This project contains 12 papers and 12 different printing techniques.

Design Agency: **atipo®** / Client: **Minke**

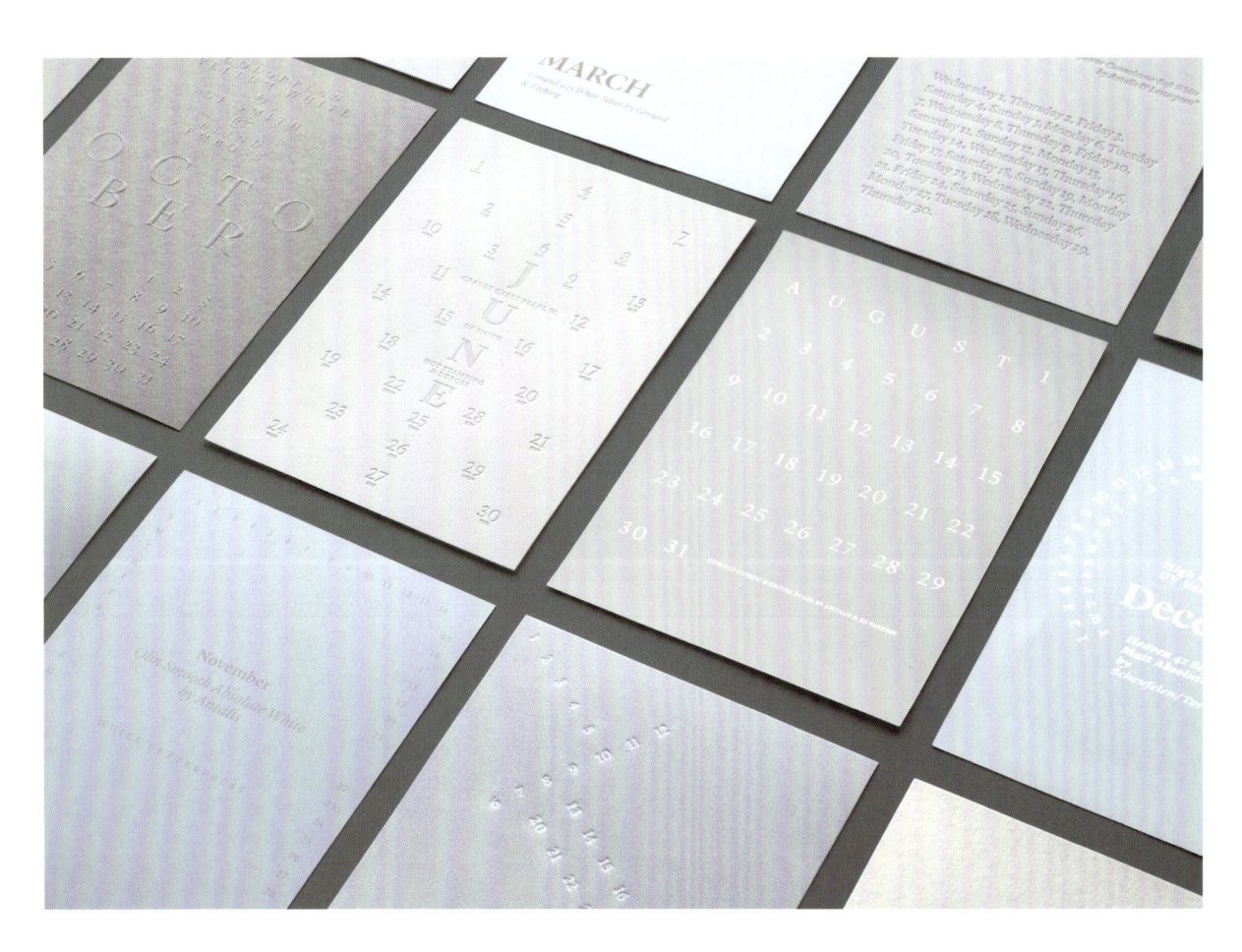

## More Letterpress Projects...

In their frigid landscape, Eskimos are able to distinguish thirty shades of white. In our warmer world, producing paper, we have found at least twelve shades. If every year has a color, 2015 looks to be a shade of white, like a blank page offering a space on which to act, to write.

Get Impressed

## Calendar 2018

Steppe Magpie brought together 12 different designers and gave them a common theme for the calendar. They limited them in colour and format and produced an interesting and very laconic product. This calendar is a decoration for any desktop.

Design Agency: **Steppe Magpie**

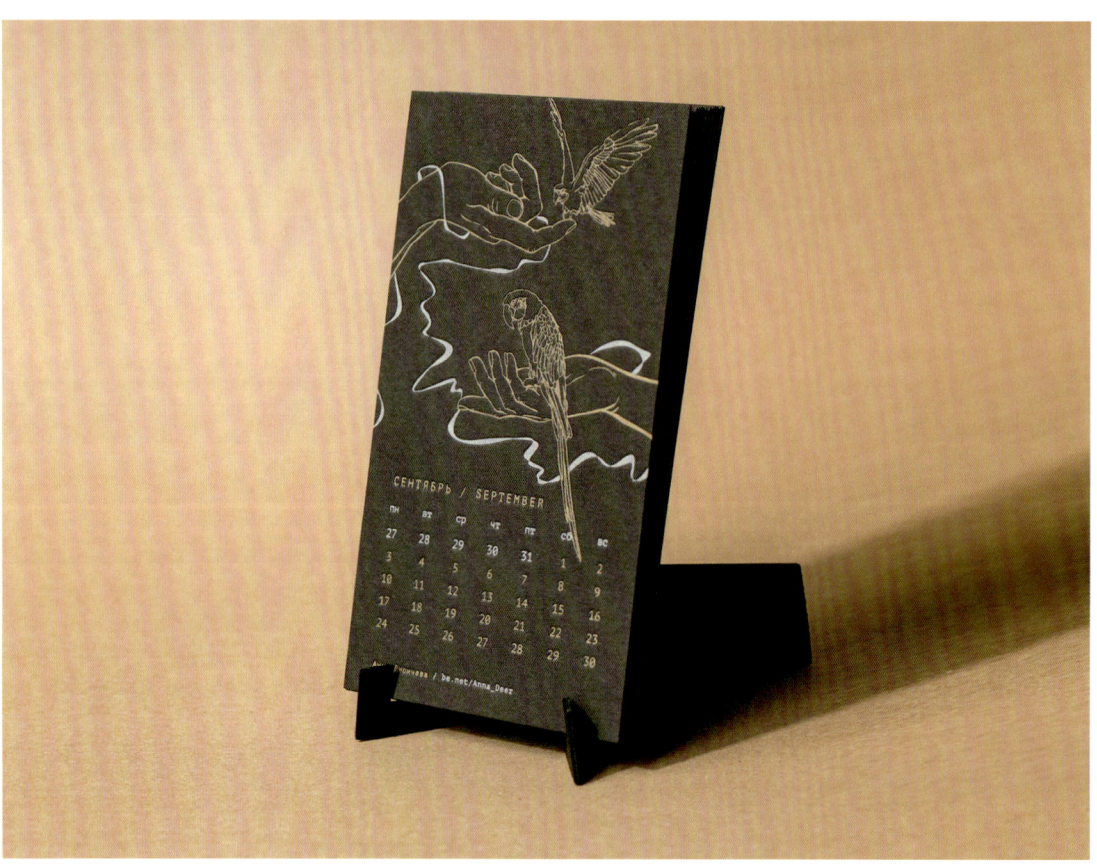

184

More Letterpress Projects...

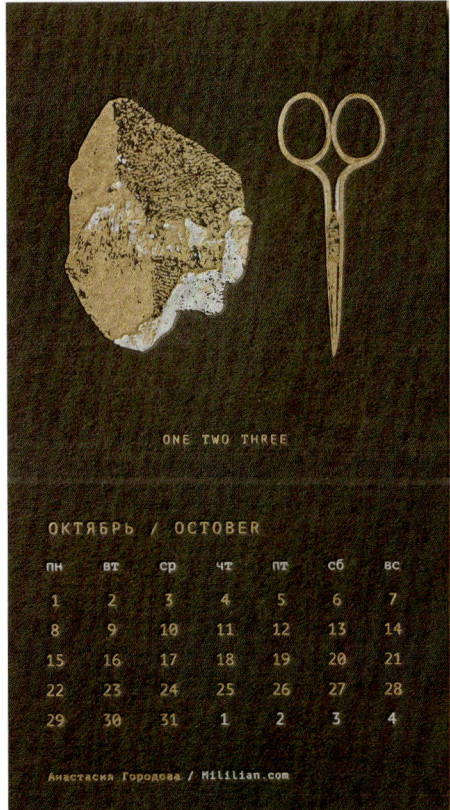

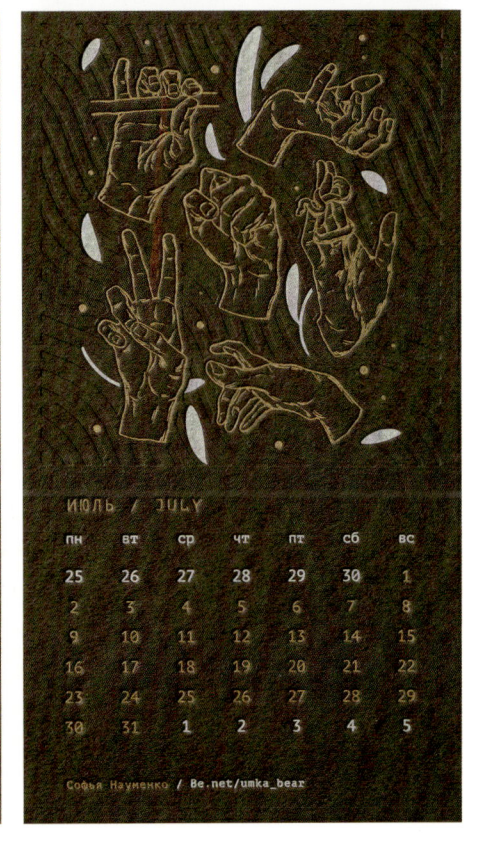

185

**Sunshine Is a Friend of Mine**

This is a poster design for Atelier Bulk.

Design: **Alexia ROUX**

## MAKE 100—Letterpress Coasters

The designer started working with letterpress printing ten years ago. It basically changes his way of designing. He creates a set of four coasters to explore possibilities. With the first printing, he creates a prototype of a wood box for a set of eight coasters, but it never goes further; only five were made to see how the box looks. To celebrate the past ten years, Mr Cup decides to reprint the original coasters, create a set of four more coasters, and an edition of 100 with the wood box as part of the MAKE 100 project.

Design: **Mr Cup**

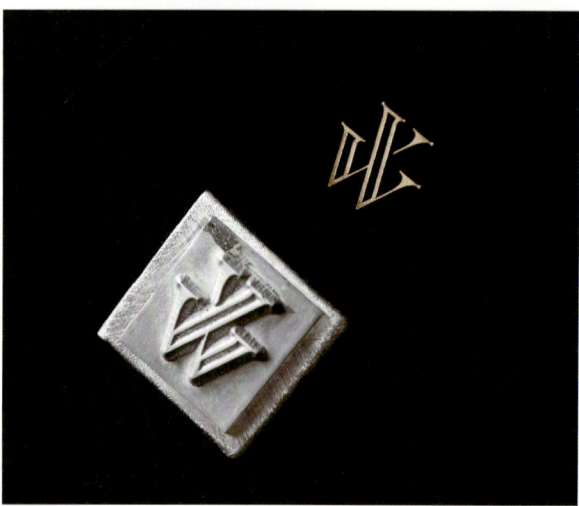

**Victor Weiss Studio Visual Brand**

At the Victor Weiss Studio, designers are passionate about the process of creating visual brands. They are determined to make every project they undertake intelligent, functional, and efficient for companies and people that look to stand out in the market. They incorporate history, values, mission statements, and icons to create sophisticated, clean, modern designs that best represent the company's concepts. Design is one of the most powerful forces in the designers' lives, whether or not they are aware of it. The designers at Victor Weiss Studio believe design can make companies succeed just as much as bad design can contribute to failure.

Design Agency: **Victor Weiss Studio** / Printing: **Letterpress Brasil** / Photography: **Fernando Cruz**

More Letterpress Projects...

## Maison Emilienne

This is a brand identity for a France-based furniture and decoration store, Maison Emilienne.

Design: **Alexia ROUX**

## Pink Holographic

This is a project for the designer's own business card.

Design: **Alexia ROUX**

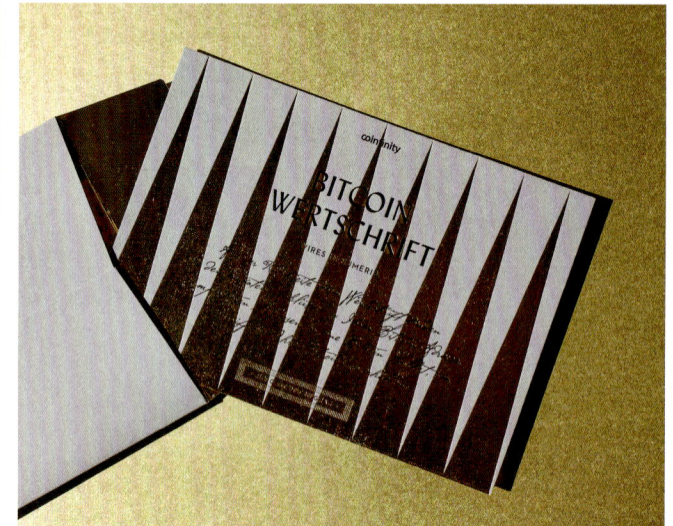

# Coinfinity

Coinfinity is Austria's leading trading partner of the cryptocurrency and payment system Bitcoin. To make a huge investment more tangible, Studio Bruch created a high-quality print product that is inspired by traditional trading paper but with a more modern approach. The elaborate manufacturing process, the combination between different papers, foils, and several finishing touches create several security features and communicate the high value of the document.

Design Agency: **Studio Bruch** / Creative Direction: **Studio Bruch** /
Art Direction: **Studio Bruch** / Letterpress: **Infinitive Factory**

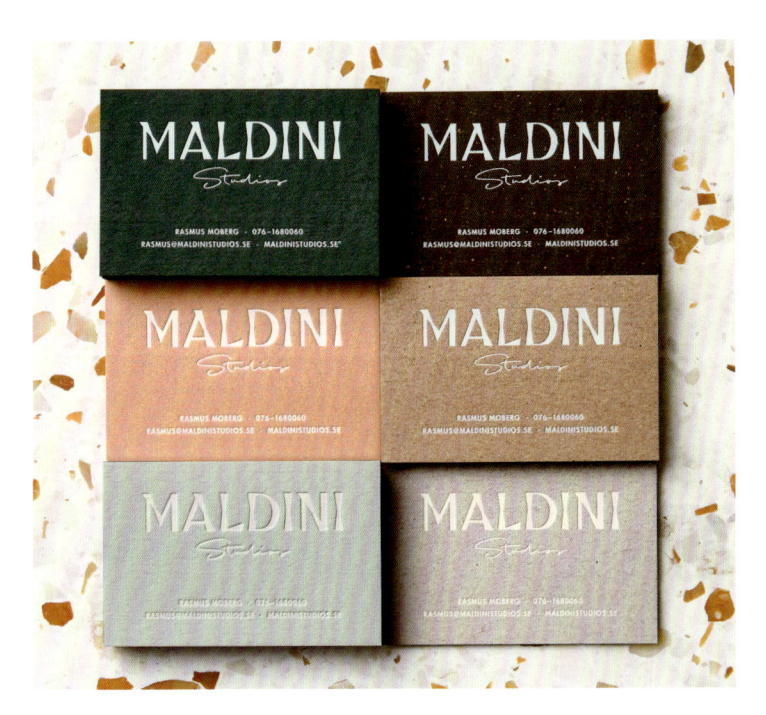

## Maldini Studios

This project is an identity for the Stockholm-based interior design and carpenter firm Maldini Studios. The studio consists of project manager and carpenter, Rasmus Moberg, interior designer Elina Johansson, and carpenter Theo Klyvare. The identity places a high focus on textures and materials with the custom-made typeface Faxi as the main component. The letterpress printed stationaries are printed on mixed textured papers from G . F Smith and Arjowiggins.

Design: **Jens Nilsson**

## Quer kommuniziert

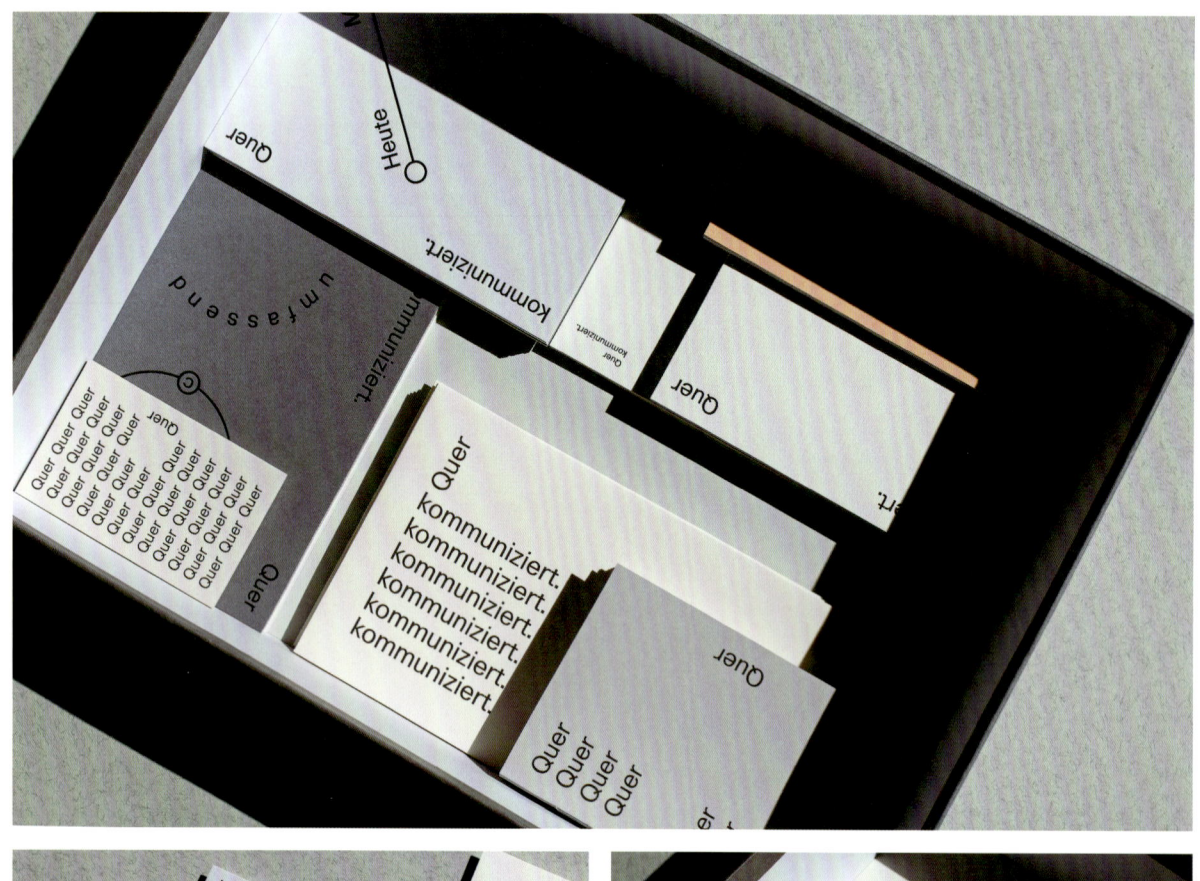

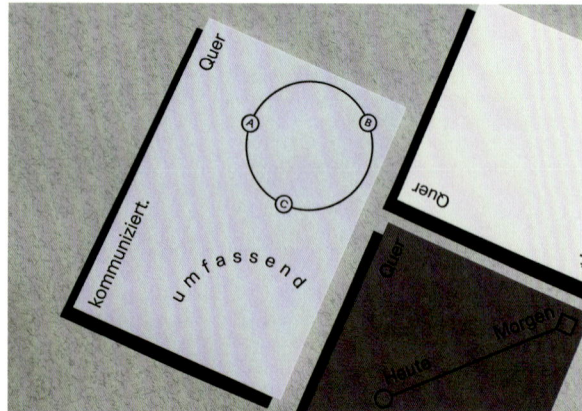

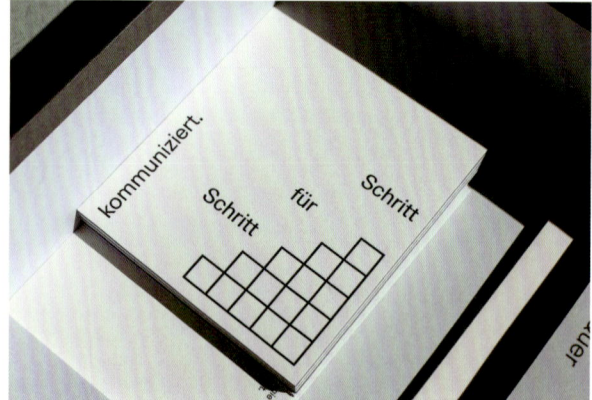

Quer kommuniziert is a holistic communication studio with a strong focus on strategy and content. The brand name as well as the work and philosophy of the studio are the starting points of the new corporate identity. Studio Bruch decided to put the content at the center of the new branding system by arranging and emphasizing text to create a unique visual style. In contrast to the clear and graphical use of type, the gentle colour palette gives the brand a friendly appearance and communicates the variety of the studio's portfolio.

Design Agency: **Studio Bruch** / Creative Direction: **Studio Bruch** /
Art Direction: **Studio Bruch** / Letterpress: **Infinitive Factory**

More Letterpress Projects...

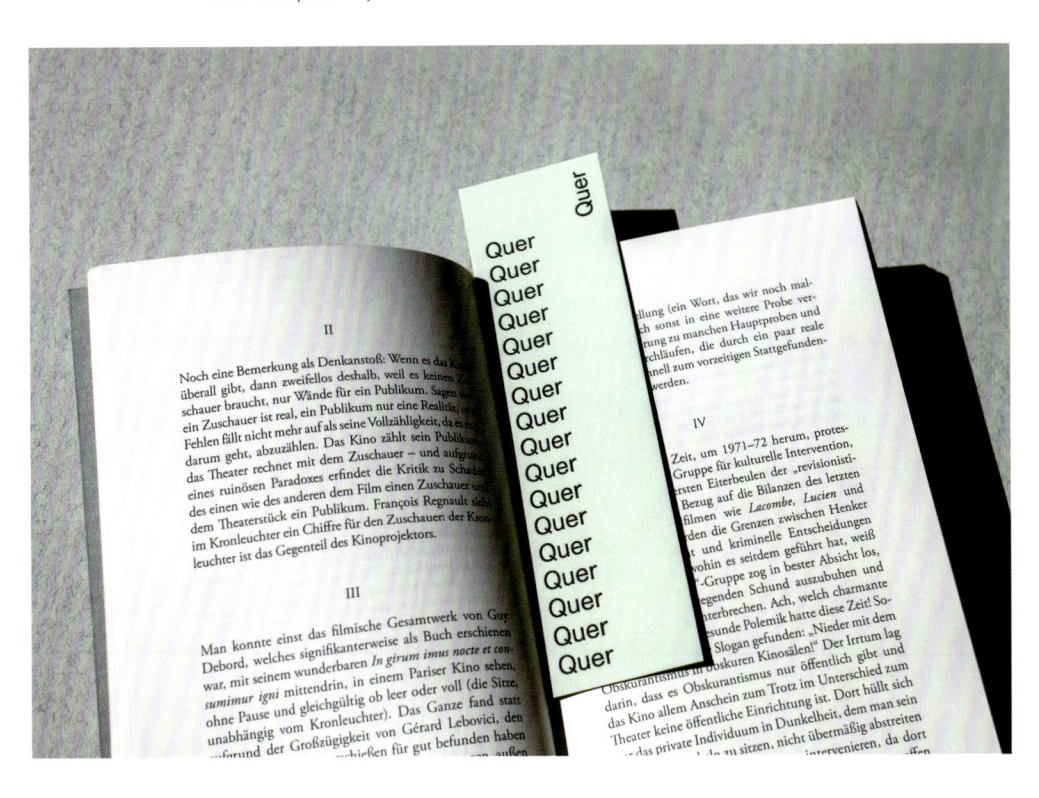

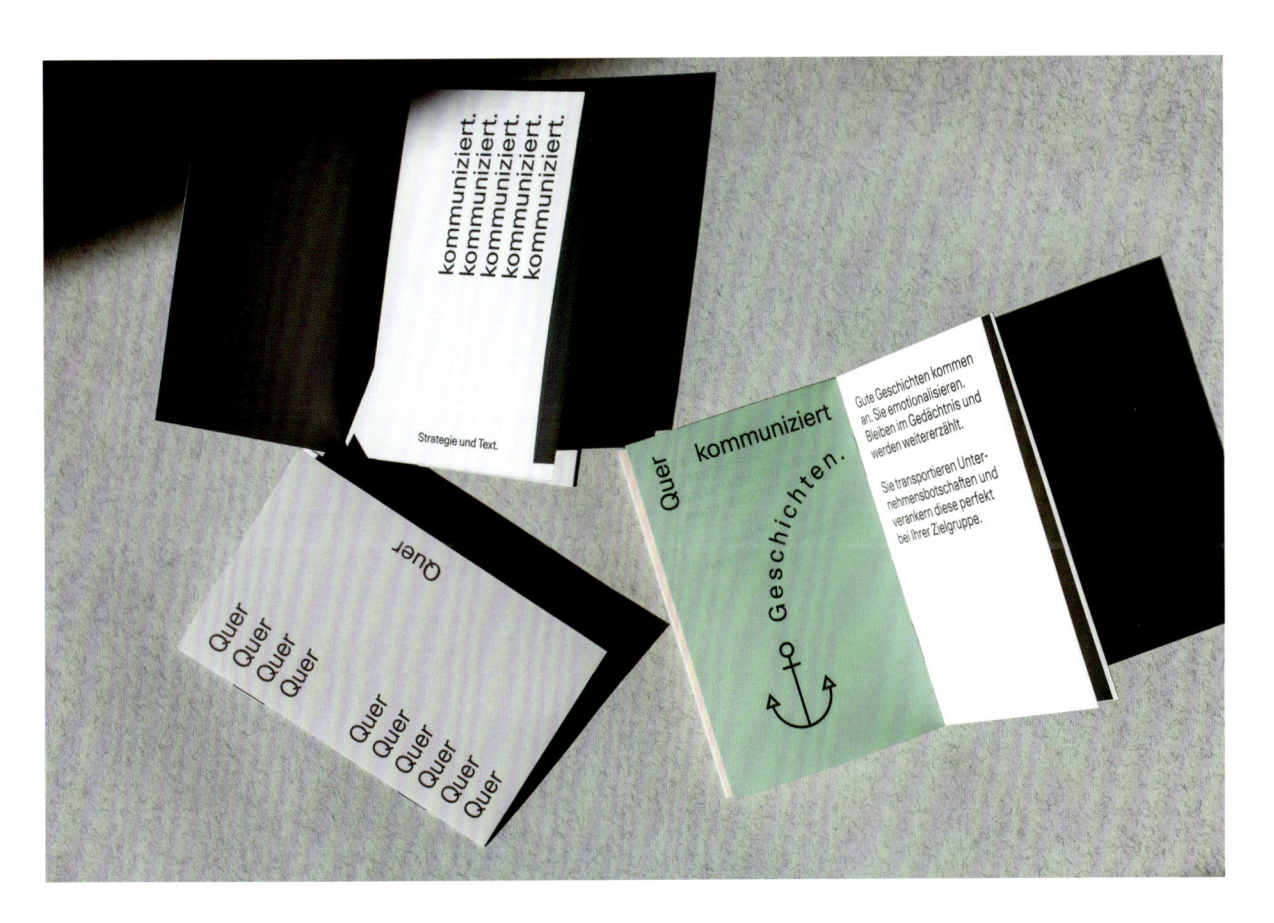

## Proclamation Whiskey

Proclamation Whiskey honors both the history and the people behind the birth of the Irish Proclamation, and the pivotal role they played at the turn of the 20th century coupled with their enduring importance in the 21st century.

Design Agency: **Backbar Studios** / Strategy: **Jason Kid** / Illustration: **David Rooney** / Photography: **Eugene Langan**

More Letterpress Projects...

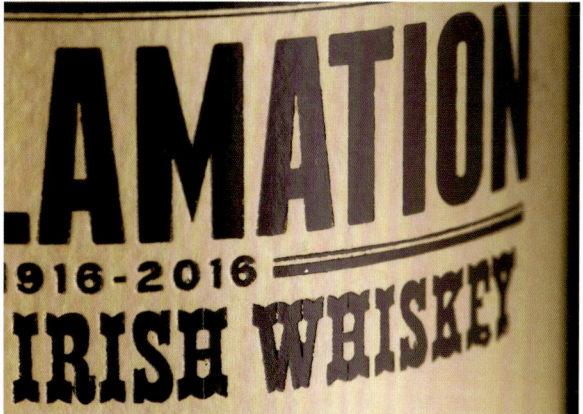

## The Work Room by Brychcy

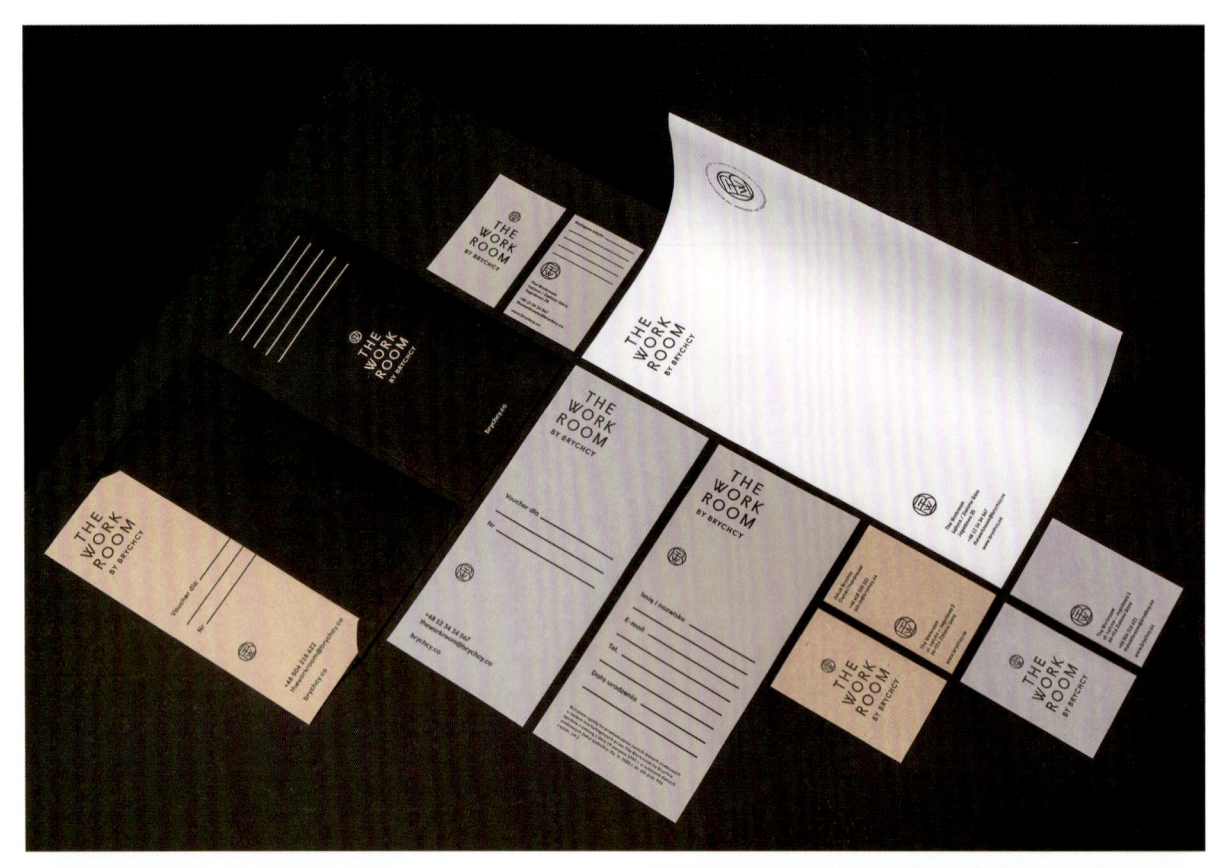

The Work Room by Brychcy is an auteur hairdressing salon founded by Jakub Brychcy, an artist and craftsman who creates haircuts inspired by the best haute couture trends as well as hairdressing traditions.

Design Agency: **Blurbstudio** / Photography: **Mateusz Wojnar**

More Letterpress Projects...

### Ben Chen Photography #3

The designer uses line elements to represent the work of a photographer. The patterns are created by hot stamping on different coloured paper which makes the design look more interesting.

Design: **Sion Hsu** / Client: **Ben Chen Photography** / Photography: **Ben Chen**

Get Impressed

**Letterpress Book**

This book tells a story about an old letterpress printing company. For the cover, the designer uses thin-line printing and integrates four stories into the picture in a graphical way. She uses aqua to convey a sense of freshness and matches it with the ancient typeface collected from Ri Xing Type Foundry. Layer by layer, the story extends to postcards, bookmarks, etc. She also adds hand-drawn objects to geometric lines to create more fun and emotion.

Design: **Connie Huang** /
Client: **Yanagibashi Publishing**

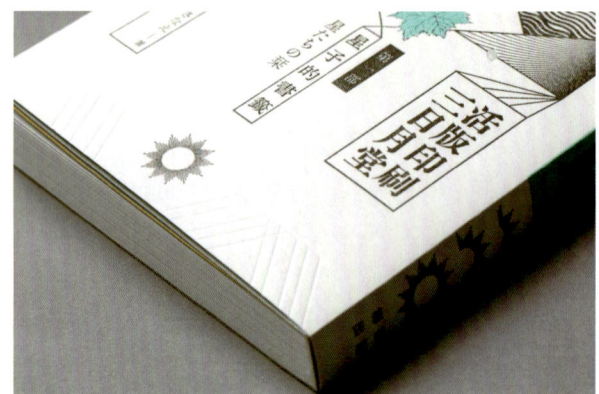

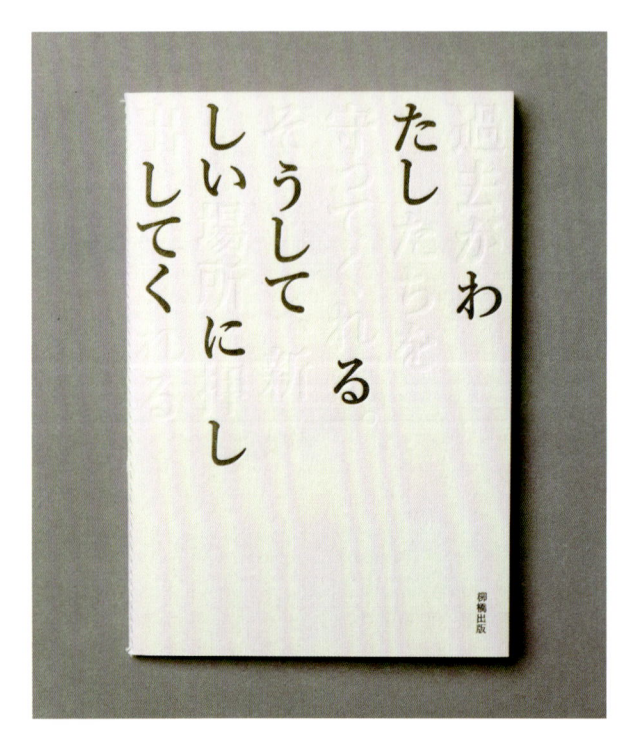

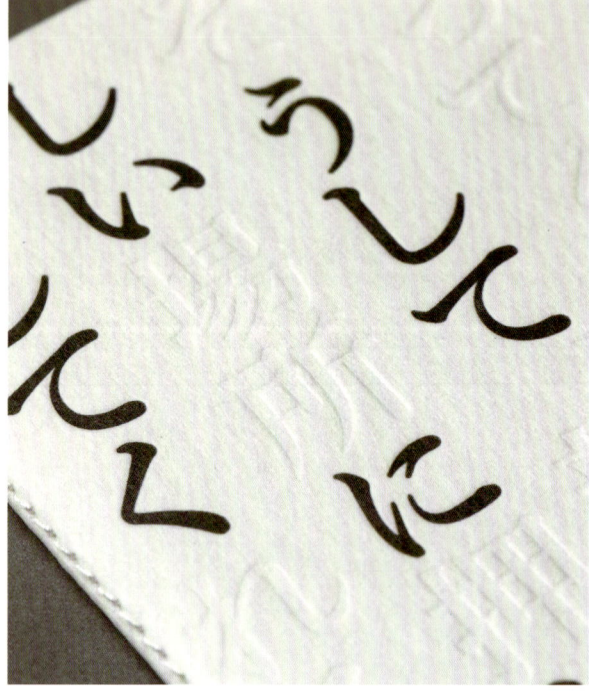

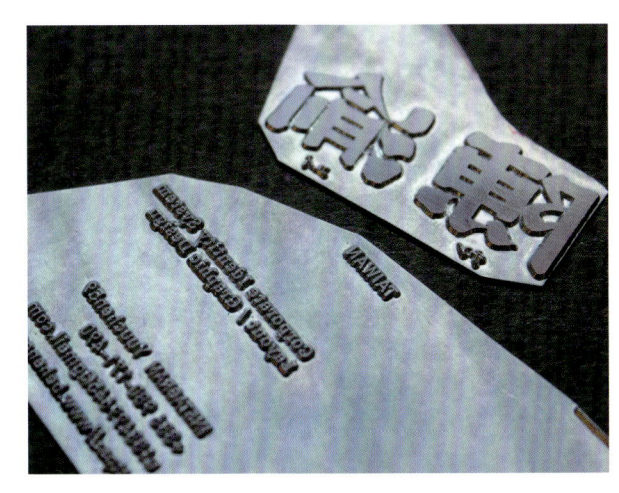

## Yu-Chen Business Card

The business card uses the paper itself with grey cardboard for post-processing. The block and black printing convey the hierarchy of information of the business card.

Design: **Yu-Chen** / Photography: **Yu-Chen**

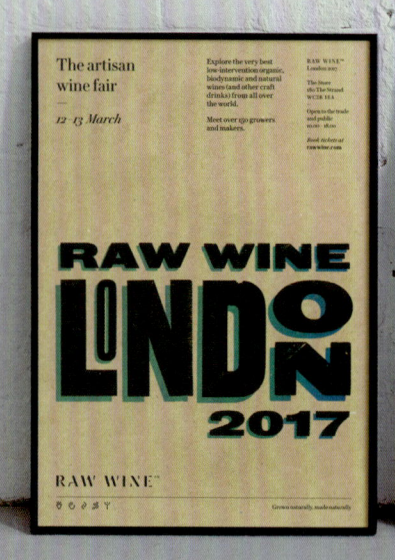

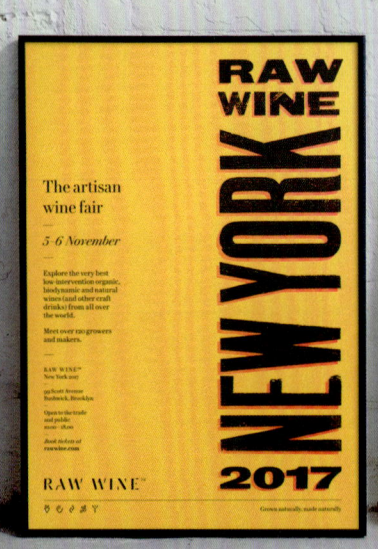

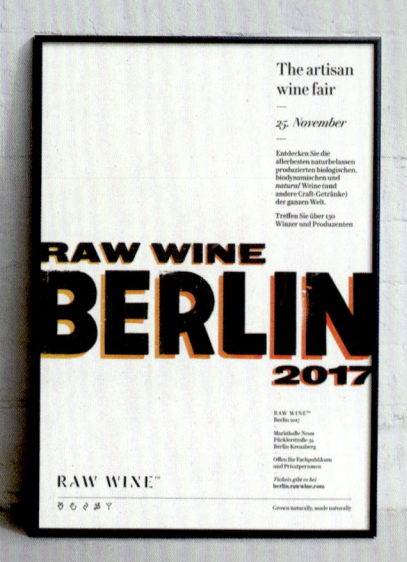

## Raw Wine

The Counter Press created a new identity that would capture both the quality and the individuality of these wines and their artisan producers. This balance is perfectly reflected in the idiosyncrasies of wood-letter typography and the crafted production of letterpress, which sits at the heart of the new brand identity. In addition, they also created a new bespoke logotype and a suite of custom icons, which represent the five fundamental principles of Raw Wine. Since the rebranding, the design studio has been working with Raw Wine to develop the identity each year for the different wine festivals around the world, through the creation of unique posters, signage, catalogs, bags and promotional materials. It is a perfect combination of traditional letterpress and modern production.

Design Agency: **The Counter Press** / Design: **Elizabeth Ellis, David Marshall** / Strategy: **Dan Rowe** / Client: **Raw Wine**

More Letterpress Projects...

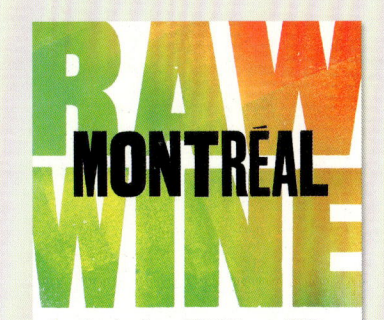

Get Impressed

## Sorry Mom Tattoo Studio

Sorry Mom is a family-owned tattoo studio of a new kind. The concept of the identity project combines elements from both handmade lettering and high-end finishing in a contemporary, yet retro-inspired style. The strikingly, bold colour blue creates a beautiful contrast with the off-white of the high-quality paper and the textures generated by the stamp. The identity echoes elements from the vintage tattoo culture while elevating it to a modern-day taste.

Design Agency: **We Are Büro Büro** /
Creative Direction: **Stefan Mückner** /
Art Direction: **Stefan Mückner** /
Design: **Sarah Scherer, Nils Zimmermann, Julian Faudt, Stefan Mückner** / Clients: **Dennis Bebenroth, Sorry Mom Tattoo Studio** /
Photography: **Thorsten kleine Holthaus, Stefan Mückner**

More Letterpress Projects...

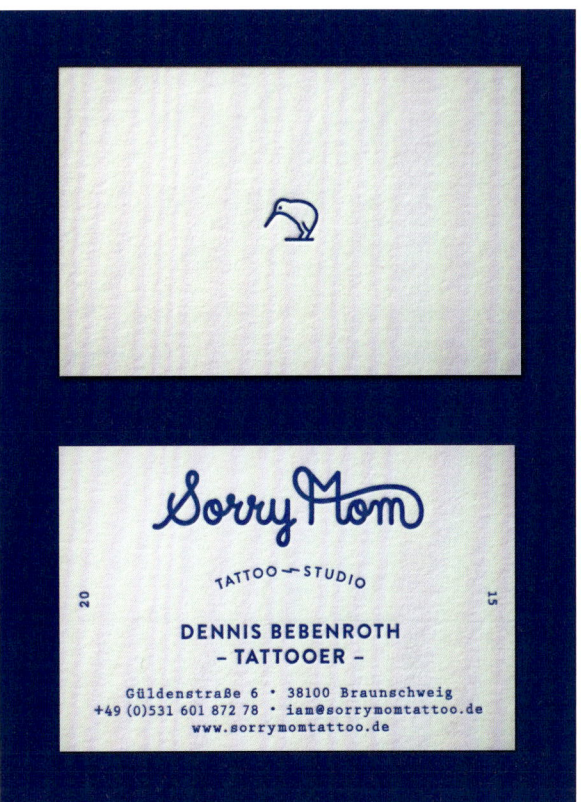

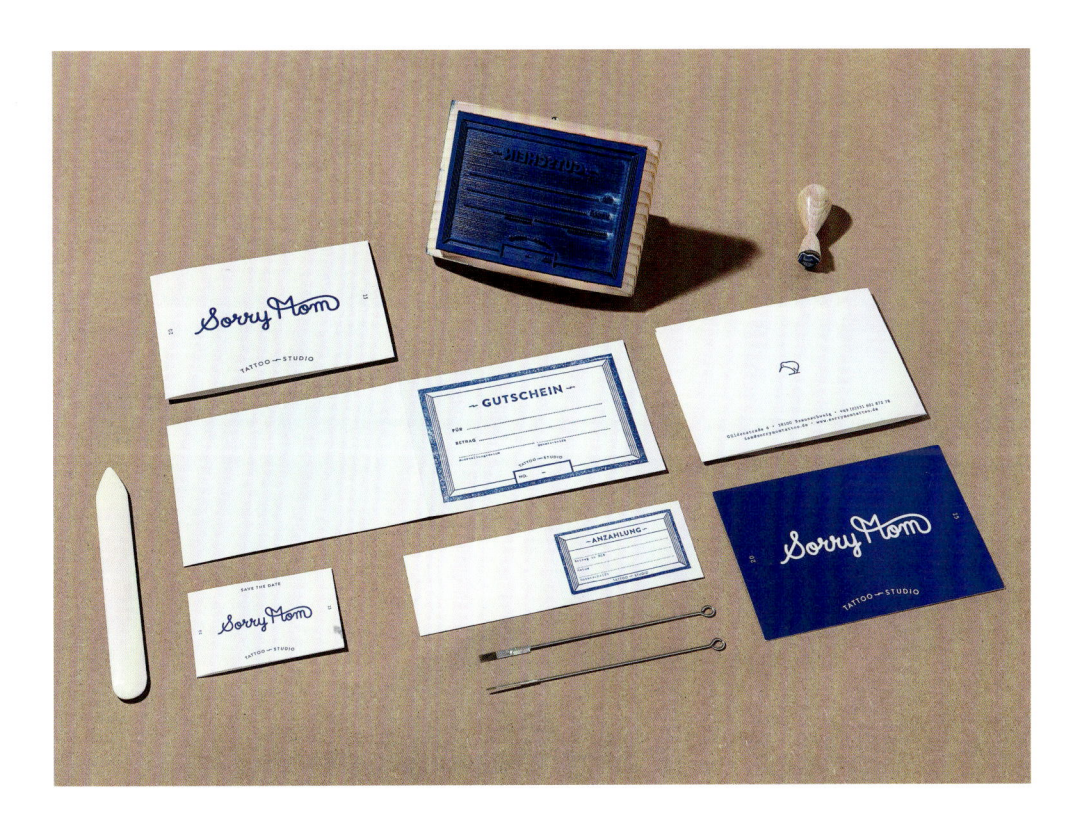

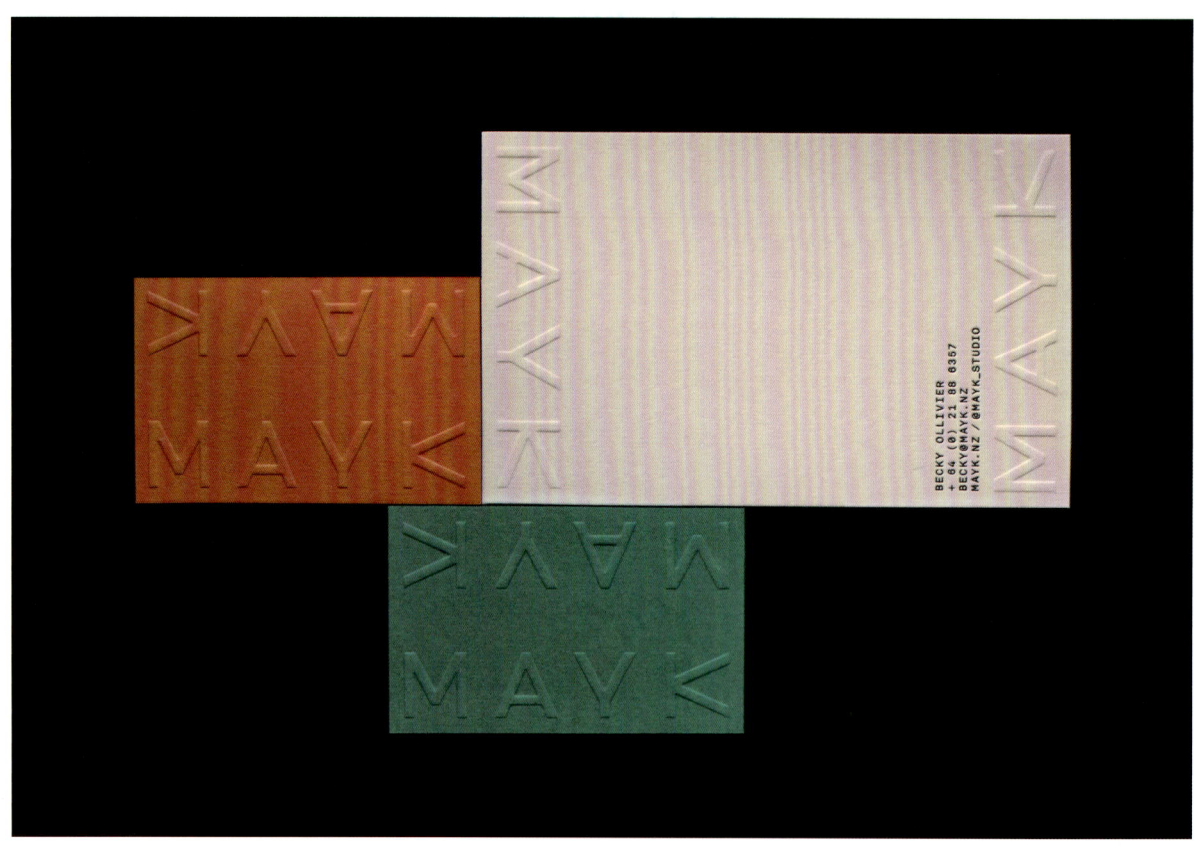

## MAYK

MAYK is an Auckland-based, independent creative studio formed by Becky Ollivier. The intention for the MAYK brand was to create a simple yet distinctive identity that represents the tactile brand values of creativity and functionality.

Design Agency: **MAYK Studio** / Art Direction & Design: **Becky Ollivier, MAYK Studio** / Printing: **Graham Judd, Inkiana Press**

More Letterpress Projects...

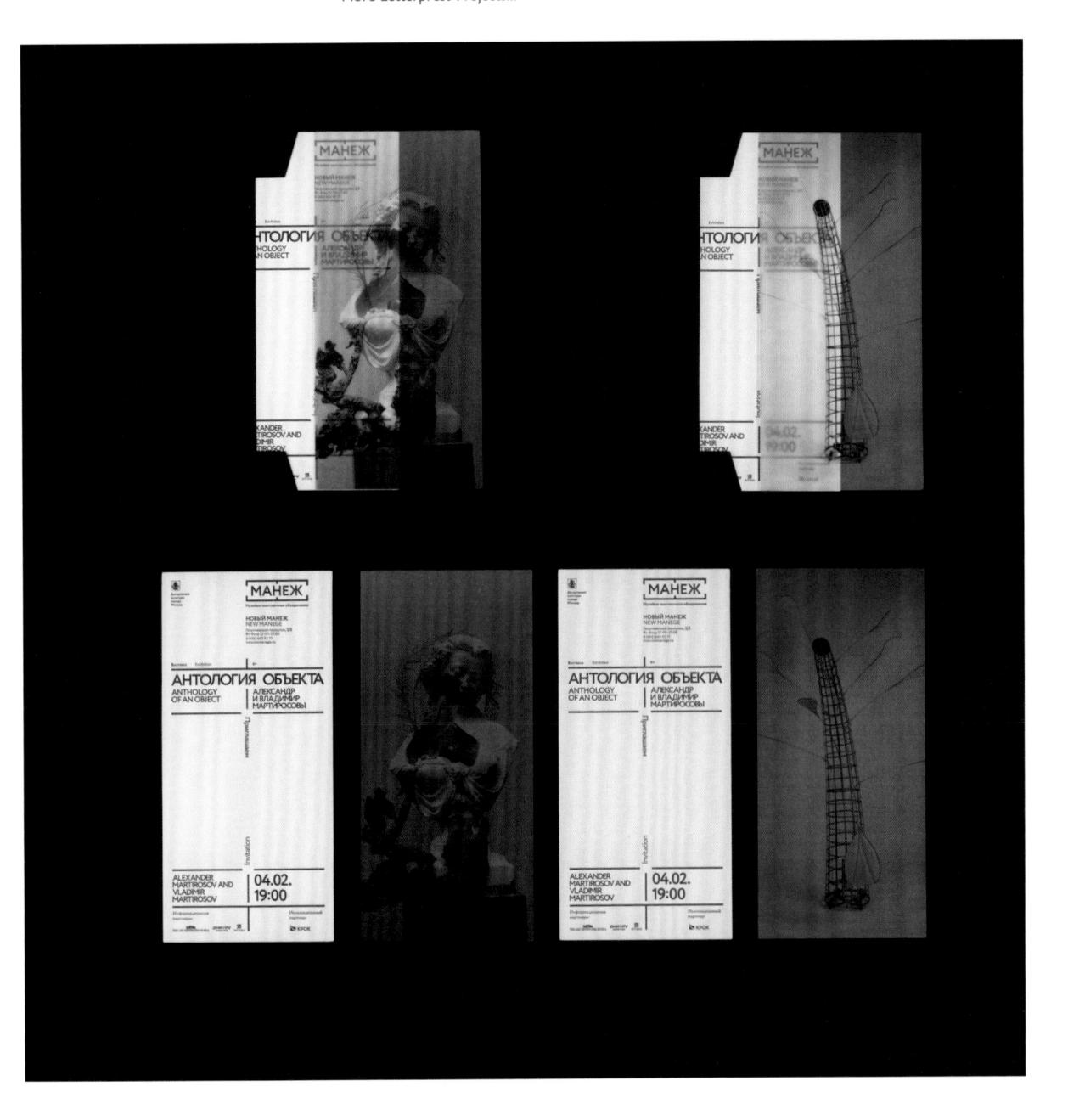

### Anthology of an Object

Besides lines and negative space, typography is the key element of the museum's identity. That's why the designer finds it crucial to treat every single word as a logotype.

The exhibition is divided into two parts, which represent the works of two artists: the father and the son. Working on the invitation design, it was important to reflect the contrast between them. The invitation consists of thick uncoated paper with letterpress and black and white photos of exhibits printed on tracing paper.

Design: **Alexander Kuliev** / Photography: **Alexander Kuliev**

## A6 Notebook

This is a series of A6 notebooks printed with vintage printing blocks from the 50–70s with platemaker names from the old days in Singapore.

Design: **Yao Yu Sun**

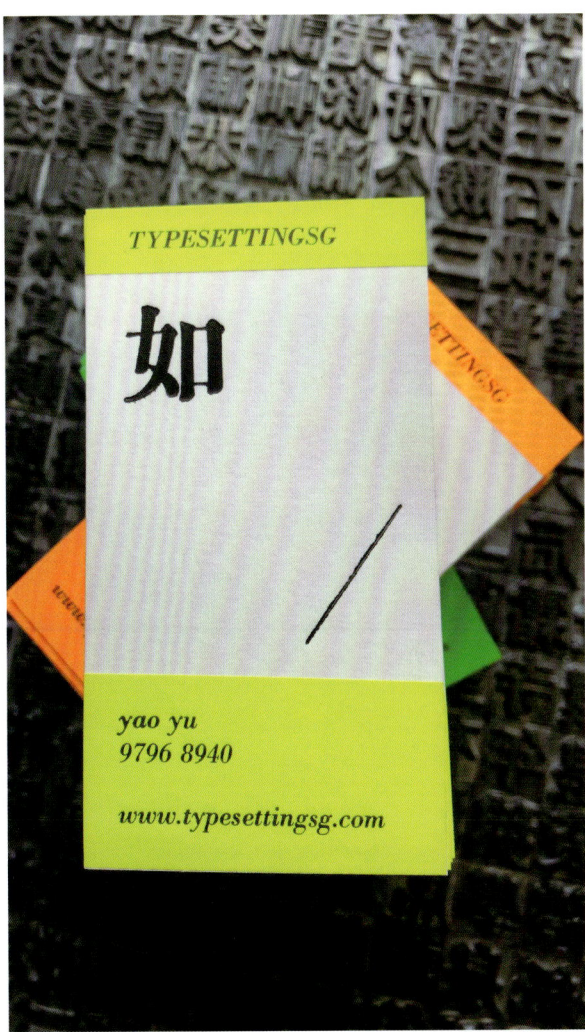

More Letterpress Projects...

### Letterpress Typeset Namecard V18

This project is printed on fluorescent stickers and on 300 gsm maple white. The fonts used are 10pt Bodoni Italic and 42pt Song Ti. Each card is printed with different Chinese characters. It is printed on a Showcard 7 x 11 Proofing Press and a Kelsey Excelsior 9 x 13 press.

Design: **Yao Yu Sun**

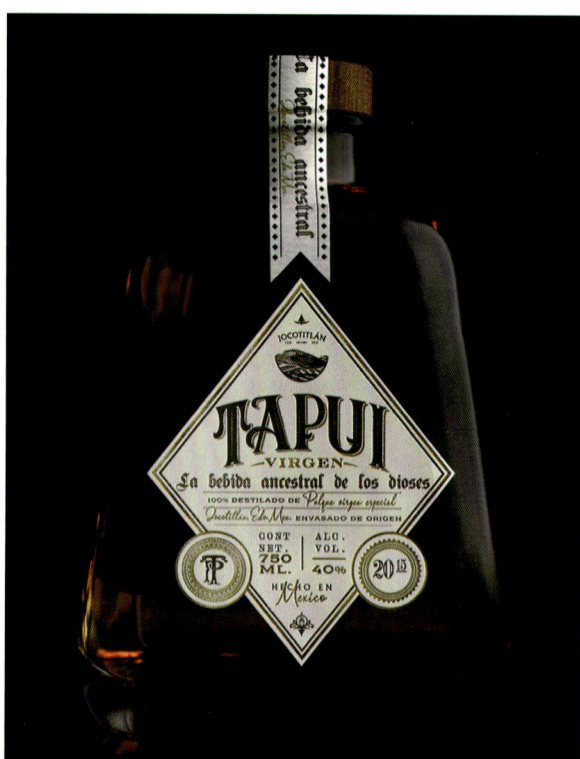

## Tapui, destilado de pulque

Tapui aims to show its artisan sense and storytelling as well as its unique thinking behind the company's brand as a family business and pulque producer. The designers pursue effective communication with their customers' clients by highlighting strong narratives.

Design: **Mauricio Arreola, Desierta.Studio, Los black lobo** /
Industrial Design: **Alejandro Santega** / Client: **Jesús Hernández y Noemí Cárdenas**

More Letterpress Projects...

### Business Card Design for Veyond

The sophisticated hot stamping adds more visual contrast to the design. Veyond's business card adopts colour foil which will vary in different angles. It is a reflection of Veyond's purpose: to introduce people into a world dazzling with attractive technology, and to bring a wonderful VR/AR realm to everyone.

Design Agency: **xonxon** / Art Direction: **xonxon** / Client: **Veyond** / Photography: **xonxon**

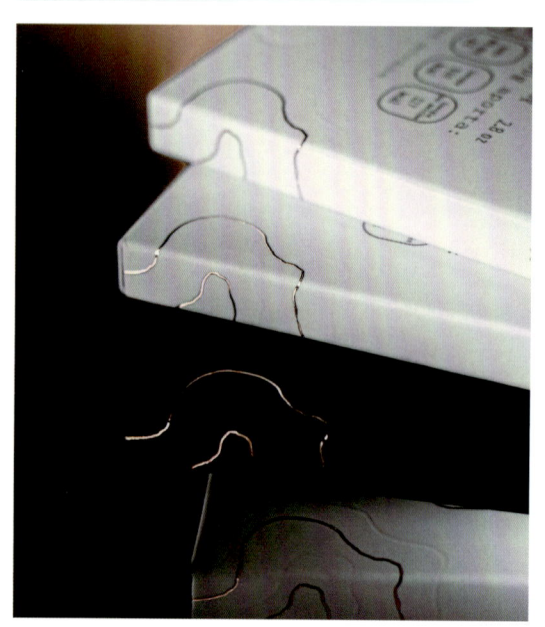

## Kinto Cacao

This project is a vision based on the exploration of the history, discipline, origins, and culture of chocolate.

Design Agency: **Desierta.Studio** / Design: **Alberto Casillas, Mauricio Arreola** / Photography: **Andrea Lizette Guardado**

More Letterpress Projects...

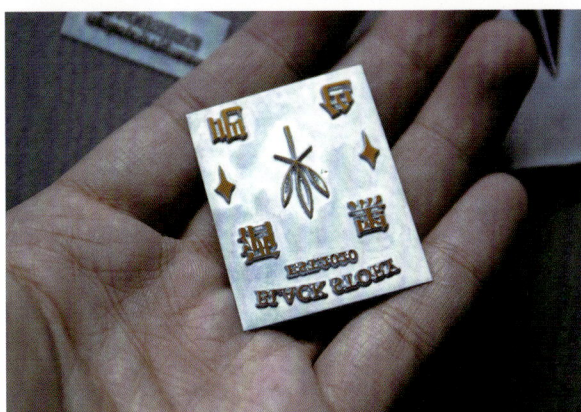

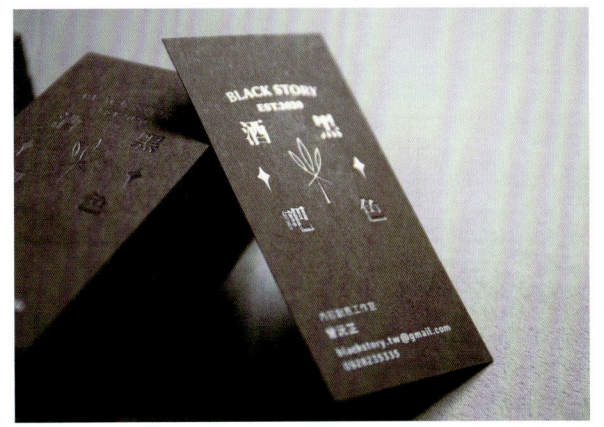

**Business Card Design for Black Story**

Black Story is a medium of horror fiction. The font that is used is about to deliver a feeling of suspense. There is a crow on the trademark logo. People are curious but also fear the unknown. The black stamp matches with the whole black colour scheme.

Design Agency: **xonxon** / Art Direction: **xonxon** / Client: **Black Story** / Photography: **xonxon**

## Pockets Full of Change

This is a design for the music band People in Houses and its album *Pockets Full of Change*. The design includes an LP sleeve (gatefold), CD cover and booklet. Together with the band, the designer decided to use a crafty approach: the illustrations were made from a linocut. To enhance the textures, the designer printed and scanned the wood type to be used for the titles and the backside. The letterpress printing took place at the designer's studio, Letterpress Corner.

Art Direction: **Armina Ghazaryan (Type & Press)** /
Design: **Armina Ghazaryan (Type & Press)** /
Client: **People in Houses**

More Letterpress Projects...

## Karol Kowalski

This branding is for photographer Karol Kowalski, including a full set of collateral, letterpress prints, and a selection of special cotton paper. The designer was looking for a typeface that would go well with the "KK" signet. He wanted to use something minimalistic but yet charismatic enough. Finally, he decided on Pluto, a simple typeface with wonderful details. It perfectly complements the logo.

Design Agency: **Foxtrot Studio** / Client: **Karol Kowalski Studio** / Photography: **Foxtrot Studio**

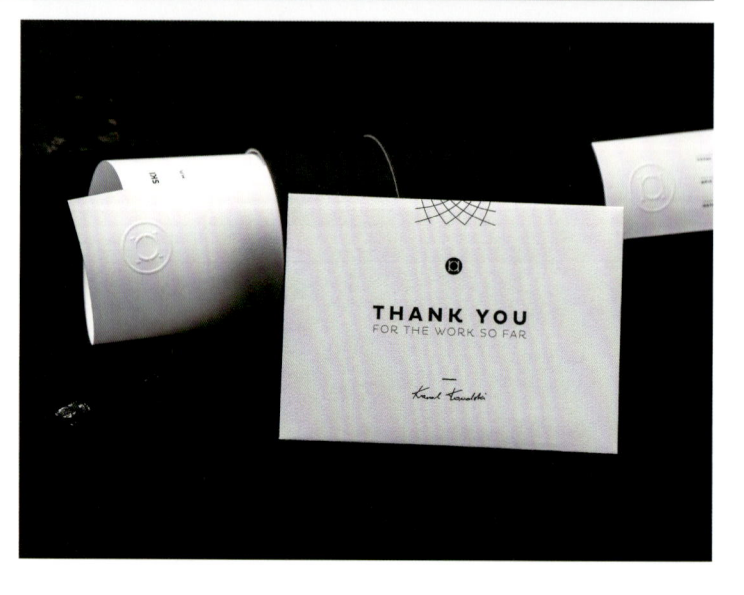

### Restore

This project is an identity design and calling card for Wanaka-based massage therapist Jane Macale. Blind deboss letterpress printed with graduating pressure emulates the effect of massage by visually restoring the card to its natural state.

Design Agency: **MAYK Studio** / Art Direction & Design: **Becky Ollivier, MAYK Studio** / Printing: **Graham Judd, Inkiana Press**

## Dream Pool of Gutenberg

Dream Pool of Gutenberg is an experimental letterpress print that tells the story of movable type from two historical perspectives. This print uses two scripts, the Roman alphabet and Chinese characters, to represent Johannes Gutenberg and Bi Sheng.

When held vertically, the print can be read in English, with the text flowing left to right. However, the reader must turn the page on its side to read the Chinese text, which flows from right to left and top to bottom. The English-language text offers a short biography of Johannes Gutenberg and his invention of movable type printing around 1450. The Chinese text is an excerpt from *Dream Pool Essays*, by the scholar Shen Kuo, who provides the earliest written account of Bi Sheng's invention of a movable type between 1041 and 1048 CE.

Design Agency: **Onion Design Associates**

More Letterpress Projects...

## JOHANNES GUTENBERG'S
# PRINTING PRESS

Johannes Gensfleisch zur Laden zum Gutenberg was a German blacksmith, goldsmith, printer, and publisher who introduced printing to Europe. His introduction of mechanical movable type printing to Europe triggered the Printing Revolution and is regarded as the most important invention of the second millennium, the seminal event which ushered in the modern period of human history. It played a key role in the development of the Renaissance, Reformation, the Age of Enlightenment, and the scientific revolution and laid the material basis for the modern knowledge-based economy and the spread of learning to the masses. Among his many contributions to printing are: the invention of a process for mass-producing movable type; the use of oil-based ink for printing books; adjustable molds; mechanical movable type and the use of a

*Gutenberg modified a screw press used for wine making.*

*Johannes Gutenberg (c.1400–1468)*

*A revolving typecase for wooden type in China, from Wang Zhen's book published in 1313.*

*Dream Pool Essays, A book written by Shen Kuo in 1088.*

*Dream Pool of Gutenberg. Designed by Onion / Printed by Ri Xing Type Foundry / Sponsored by Department of Cultural Affairs, Taipei City Government*

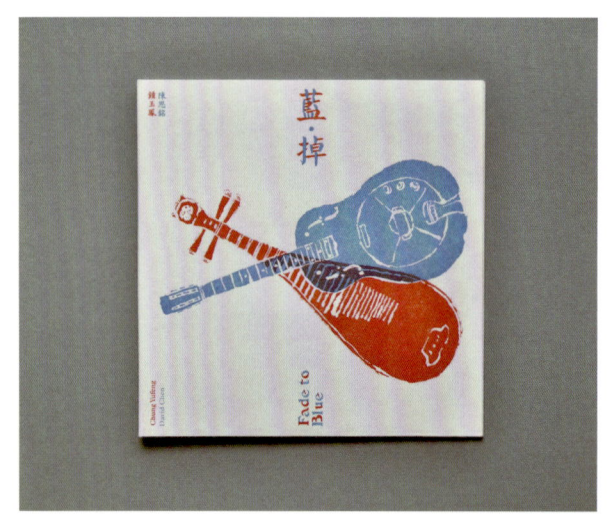

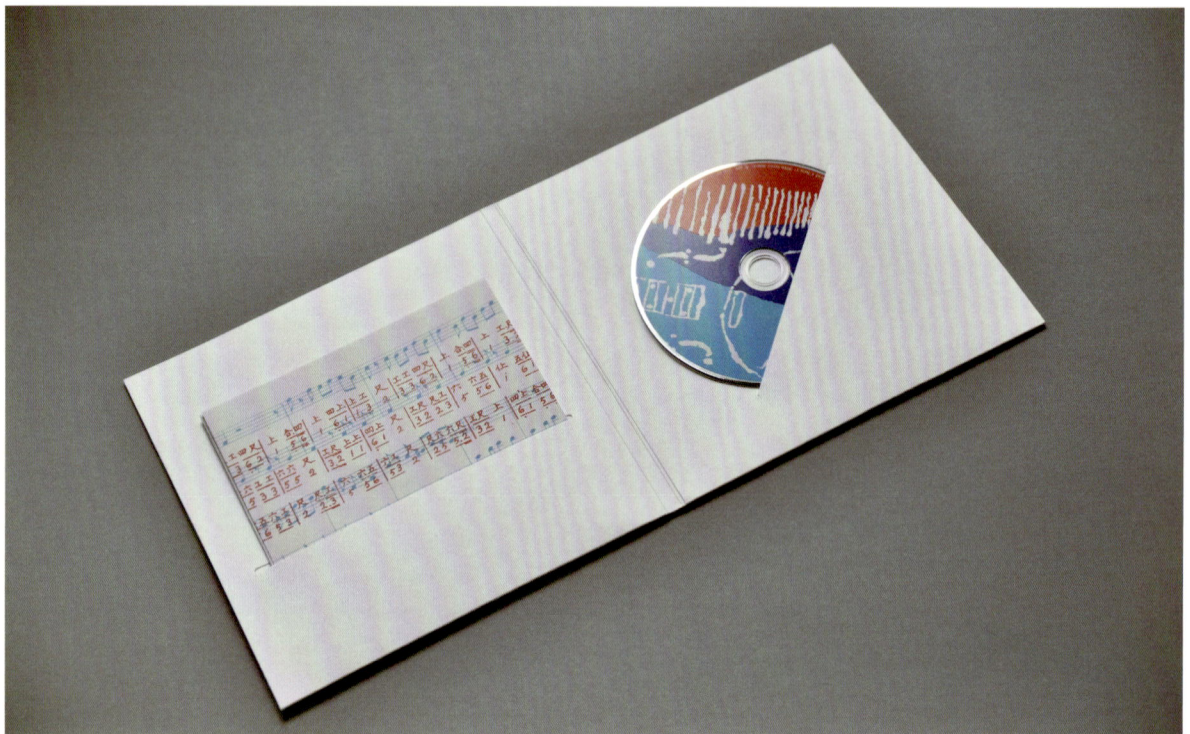

## Fade to Blue

Chung Yufeng, a pipa player, and David Chen, a US-born blues guitarist, combined the unlikely sounds of Chinese pipa and blues guitar in a collaborative music project called Fade to Blue.

Two colours (inks) were used on the entire album: red ink for the pipa, the female musician, the east; while blue ink represented the blues guitar, the male and also all the English text he wrote. Letterpress printing is also used to reinforce the raw and organic nature of their performance.

Design Agency: **Onion Design Associates**

More Letterpress Projects...

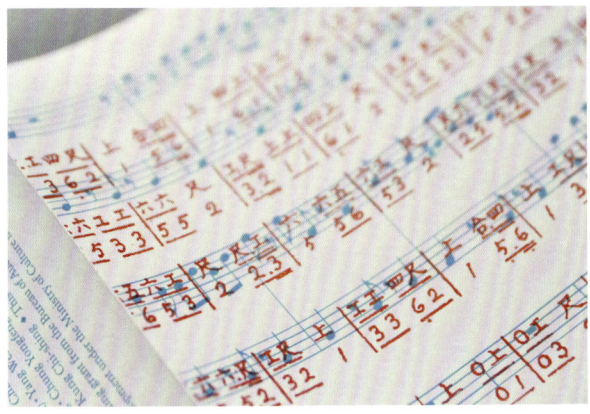

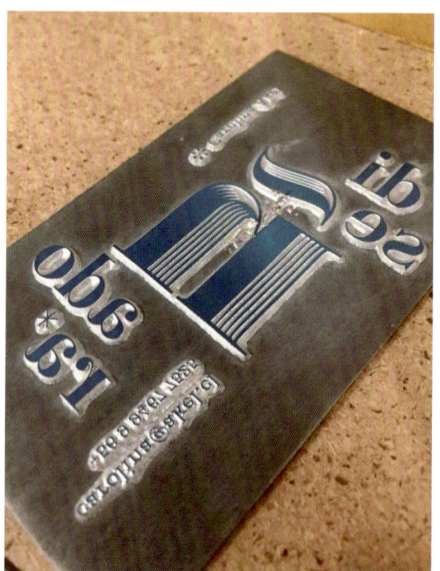

## Tarjetas Letterpress

This is a project for the designer's own business card. The idea was to use only letters as she is an editorial designer, so Obsidian typeface was perfect for making the most out of letterpress.

Design: **Carolina Akel** / Letterpress: **Alberti.cl**

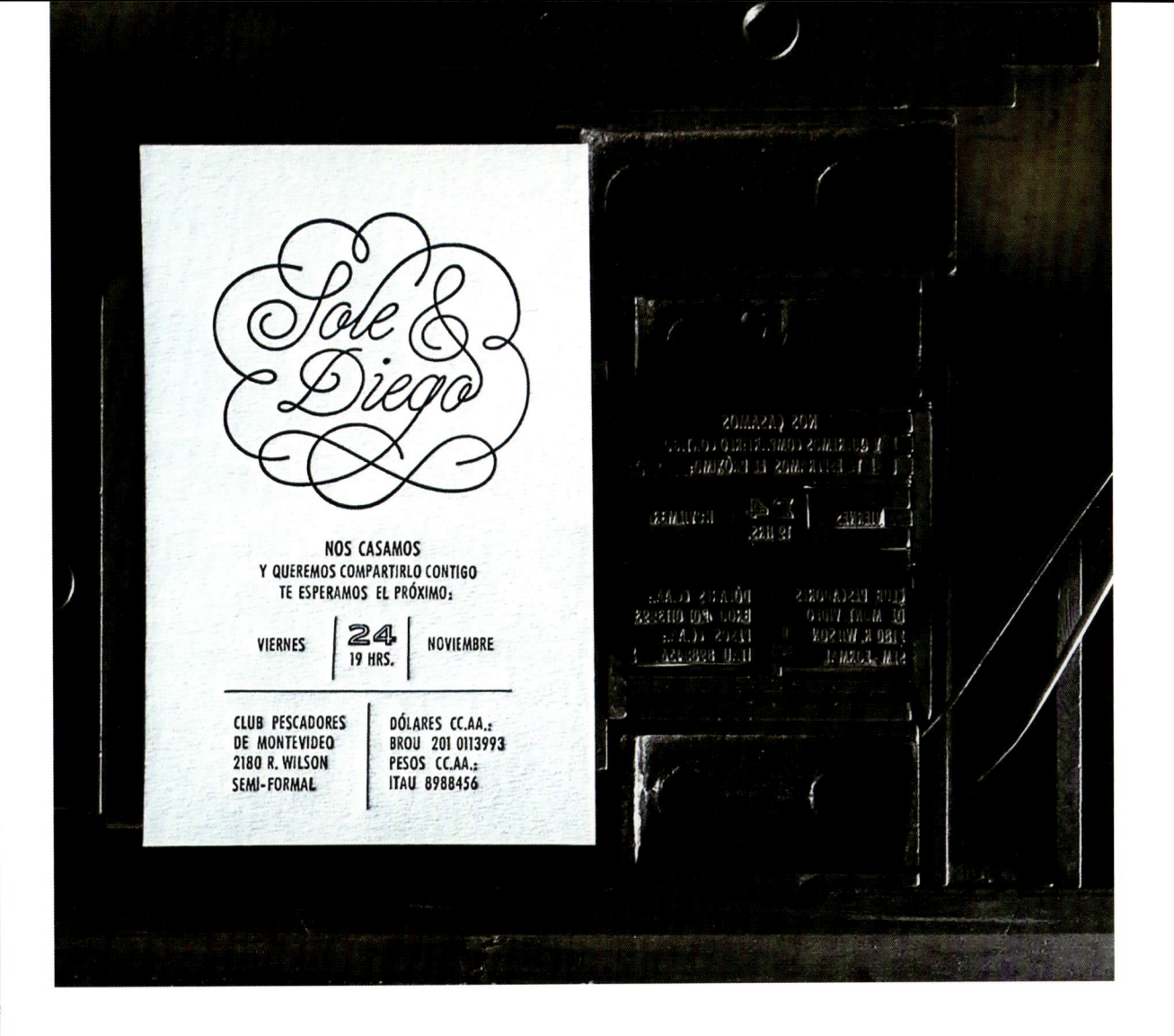

### Sole & Diego, Wedding Invitations

This project was special to the designer because it was his brother's wedding invitation cards. He designed the general layout and lettering and printed them in the Caja Baja letterpress shop, which is run by Gabrel Pasarisa. Gabrel helped to transform the digital file into movable type by using cotton paper. Finally, all the envelopes were done by the designer's hand.

Design: **Fernando Díaz** / Lettering & Calligraphy: **Fernando Díaz** / Letterpress: **Gabriel Pasarisa** / Photography: **Luciana Machin**

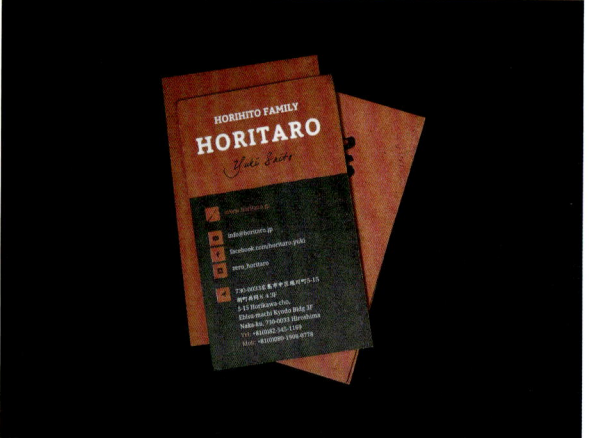

## Horitaro Tattoo Studio

Yuki Saito (a.k.a. Horitaro) is a talented tattoo artist. This project is his new business cards and shop cards. The designer asked him if she could use one of his drawings as a graphic element. He came back the next day with a beautiful ink drawing of a Koi Carp he had made during the night. When she asked him how he envisioned his communication tools, he imagined something more classy, conveying the traditional elements of his art.

Having seen Judith's then design agency's business cards printed on thick paper with letterpressed characters, he asked for the same kind of finish. He was very pleased with the idea of using only white (the paper colour), black (as the tattoo ink), and vermilion which is the colour traditionally used in the Japanese Shinto religion and in lacquerware as well as to ward off demons. Printing in two colours also reduce the cost of printing.

Design Agency: ジュディー DESIGN / Design: **Judith Cotelle** / Ink Drawing: **Horitaro** / Calligraphy: **The First Horihito** / Client: **Horitaro** / Photography: **Judith Cotelle**

More Letterpress Projects...

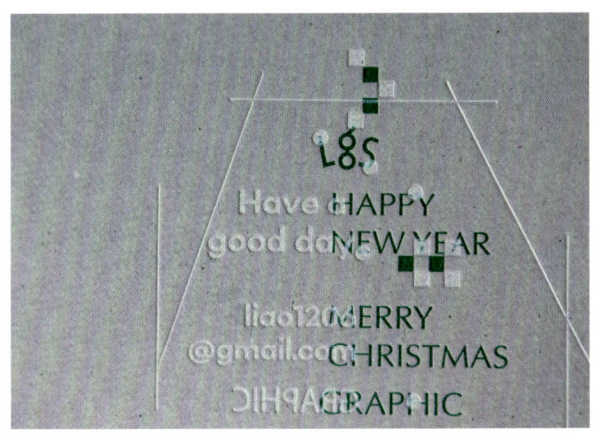

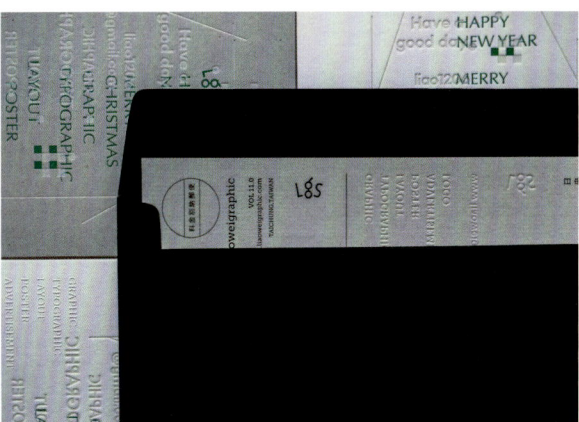

## Xmas and New Year Card 2020–2021

This is a card design for L/g/s Studio. The designer used various typefaces, colours and geometric images. The designer selected GA Kraft Board and SNOBLE paper from TAKEO Co., Ltd. On the Kraft Board, the green he used was Pantone 7479U, and before the ink dried, he overprinted multiple times with white ink.

Design: **Liao Wei** / Printing: **Sunrise Letterpress**

## Music in Print Collection

Gráfica Saúde Sá is a family-run company established in 1958 and based in Matosinhos, Portugal. They specialise in a wide variety of printing services. The Music in Print Collection creatively explores the company's available printing and finishing techniques with a musical-based concept. A selection of eight artists and their respective music tracks were chosen to be illustrated and finished with great attention to detail and workmanship. The full compilation of 120 mm × 200 mm cards which celebrate the motto, "Keep print alive", is to be offered to clients and designers that employ the company's services.

Art Direction: **Oscar Maia** / Design: **Oscar Maia** / Client: **Gráfica Saúde Sá**

More Letterpress Projects...

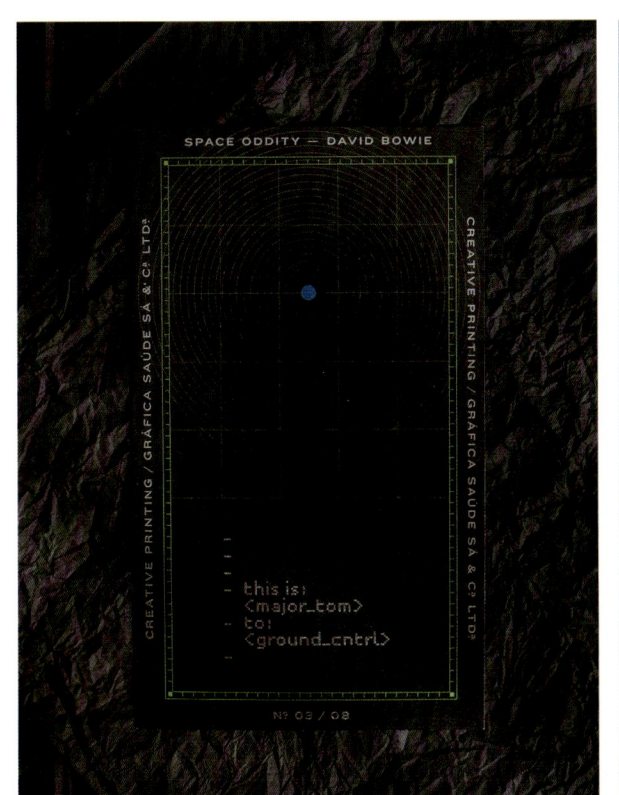

## Keiros Estilistas

Keiros Estilistas is a beauty parlor with over 15 years' experience and focuses on providing high-quality hairstyling and makeup services. The rebranding was intended to reflect their obsession with excellence in the simplest way possible; the use of black and white with vintage gold elements replaces the grey and pink palette from the original branding, together with very specific typographic curation and a custom pattern, all of which help create objects that look and feel worth having.

Design Agency: **vegrande**®

More Letterpress Projects...

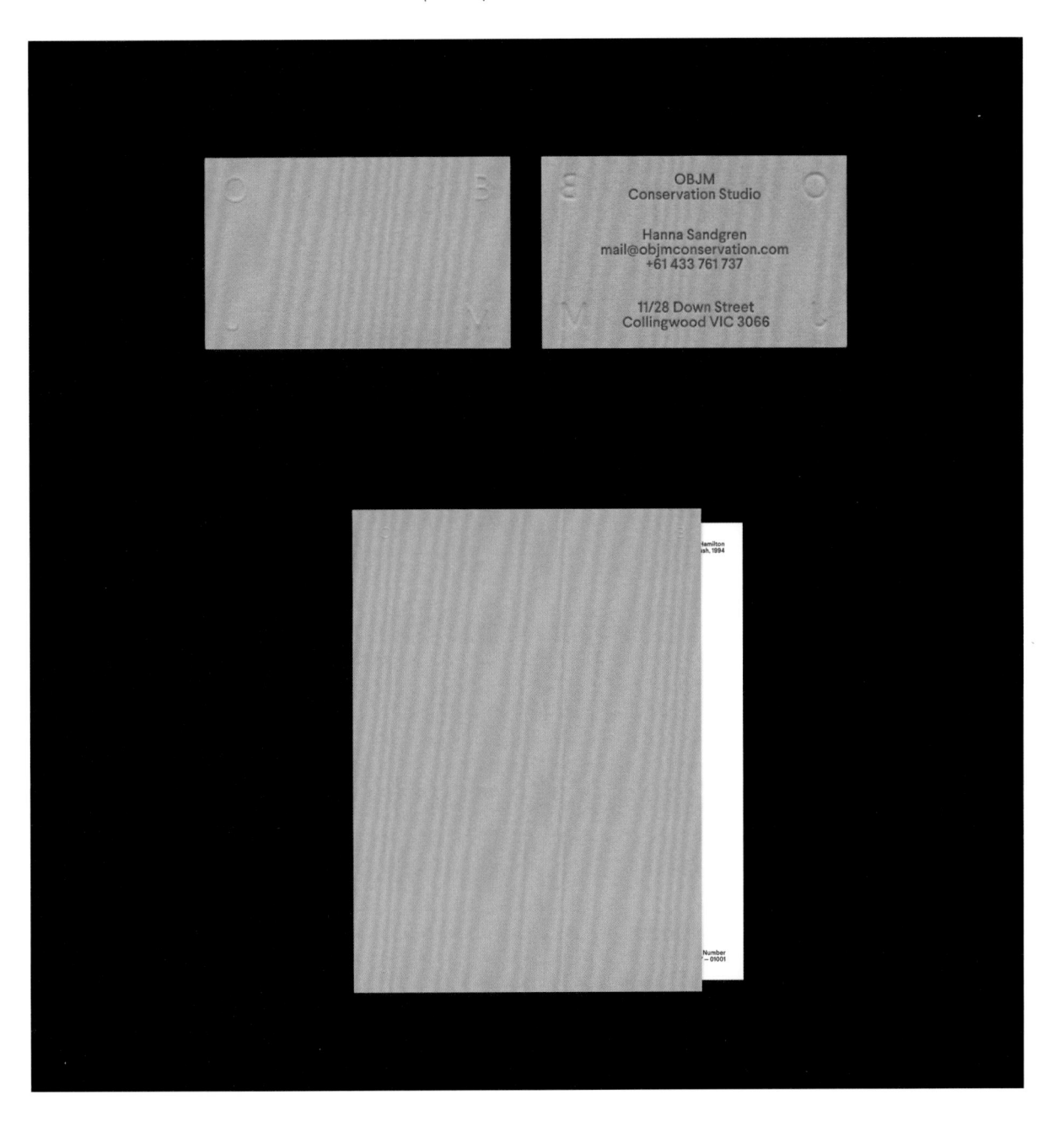

**OBJM Conservation Studio**

This project is for a Melbourne-based studio specialising in art conservation and restoration services.

Design Agency: **Susu Studio** / Printing: **Hungry Workshop**

## A Book of Helium

This is an artist's book created without a touch of ink. It is a work of celebrating traditional and modern printing techniques. The artist embraces blind emboss letterpress and digital laser cutting techniques to portray the intangible quality of helium.

Design: **Hsin-Yi Michelle Huang** / Photography: **Hsin-Yi Michelle Huang**

More Letterpress Projects...

## Prince Dining Room

Susu Studio focused on creating a set of tactile pieces that were both beautifully crafted and recyclable—addressing the often wasteful nature of single-use menus, coasters, etc. The solution starts with these wine list covers and bill folders. This is a team effort with custom hand-made stocks by Dodgy Paper, assembled and foil stamped by OrtBindery in St Kilda. Menus and coasters are printed on recycled stock from Ball & Doggett. Once the covers are shabby and worn out, Dodgy Paper will pulp them back into fresh stock along with all the menus, coasters (luxuriously letterpressed by Hungry Workshop Letterpress), and other scraps.

Design Agency: **Susu Studio** / Printing: **Hungry Workshop**

# INDEX

## ALAN KITCHING
**London, UK**
www.thetypographyworkshop.com

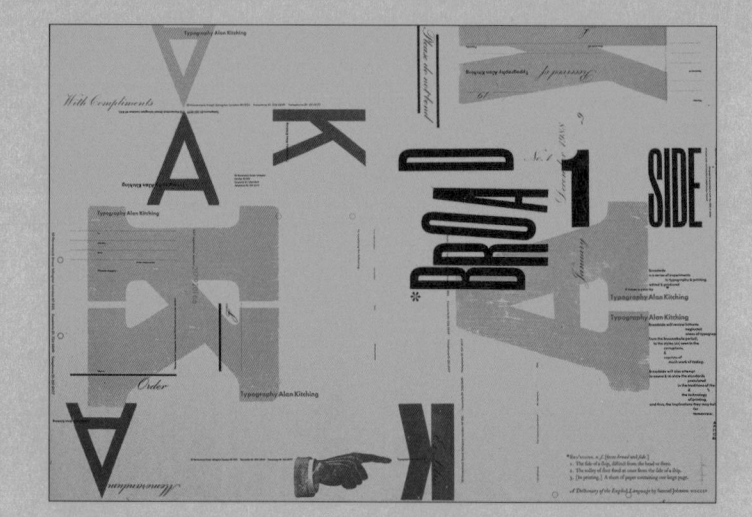

P022–031

## DAVID WOLSKE
**Denton, Texas, USA**
www.david-wolske.com

P032–041

## TOM BOULTON
**Sussex, UK**
www.typetom.com

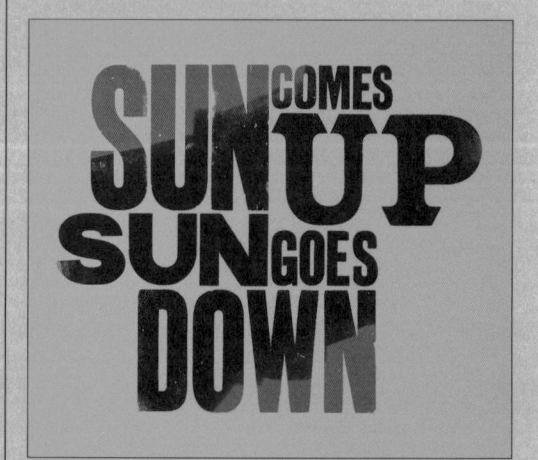

P042–049

Index

## JESSICA SPRING
Tacoma, Washington, USA
www.springtidepress.com

P050–059

## CHRIS CHANDLER
Portland, Oregon, USA
www.neuhauspress.com

P070–081

## BART HEESEN
Helden, The Netherlands
www.karakterprints.nl

## BRAD VETTER
Louisville, Kentucky, USA
www.bradvetterdesign.com

P060–069

P082–094

# CLAWHAMMER PRESS
**British Columbia, Canada**
www.clawhammer.ca

*P096–107*

# TIPOTECA ITALIANA
**Cornuda, Italy**
www.tipoteca.it

*P108–119*

# GINGERLY PRESS
**Pittsburgh, Pennsylvania, USA**
www.gingerlypress.com

*P120–129*

# P98A
**Berlin, Germany**
www.p98a.com

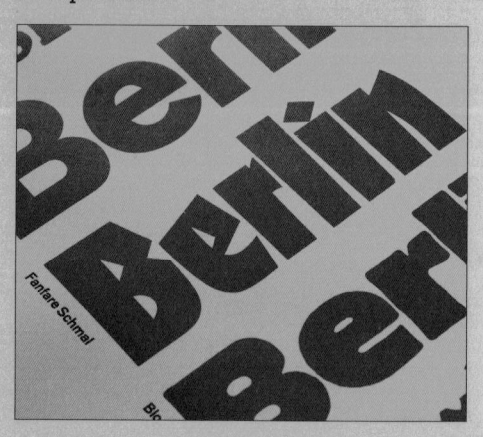

*P130–137*

Index

## RI XING TYPE FOUNDRY
**Taiwan, China**
www.facebook.com/rixingtypefoundry

P138–145

## THE SCHOOL OF BAD PRINTING
**USA/Argentina/The Netherlands**
www.kennedyprints.com
www.robarragan.com.ar
www.mizdruk.nl

P146–159

## NORTH OR NOWT
**Leeds, UK**
www.northornowt.com

P160–170

## Alexander Kuliev

Alexander Kuliev is a Moscow-based independent graphic designer.

www.behance.net/iAck-Nolev

P207

## Alexia ROUX

Alexia ROUX is a graphic designer based in Montpellier. She designs and develops visual identity projects.

www.alexiaroux.fr

P180–181, 186, 190–191

## Armina Ghazaryan

Armina Ghazaryan is an Armenian-born freelance graphic designer and a letterpress practitioner based in Ghent, Belgium. She is the founder of Letterpress Corner printmaking studio in Ghent with a primary focus on letterpress workshops for groups and individuals who would like to acquire a practical knowledge of this craft. Her works are featured in various publications by Gestalten, Rockport, Rotovision and BIS publishers. In 2008, she joined the printing team of the Museum of Industry (Ghent, Belgium) where she designs and typesets posters using wood and metal type as well as catalogs the museum's wood type collection.

www.typeand.press

P214–215

## atipo®

atipo® is a small studio located in Gijón (in the Asturias region of northern Spain), which was founded by Raúl García del Pomar and Ismael González in 2010. They met while studying Fine Arts at the University of Salamanca. After working in other graphic design, web design and branding studios, they thought it was time to launch a personal project that allowed them to develop the work from a personal point of view. Their background in Fine Arts allows them to experiment with and combine different disciplines (typography, photography, painting, illustration and video) as they produce each work. Their projects have seen the light in numerous publications and have garnered professional distinctions, such as earning Laus Awards, Motiva Awards, Brandemia, Gràffica, Brand New Awards and European Design Awards.

www.atipo.es

P182–183

## Backbar Studios

Backbar Studios has quickly built a reputation as a dedicated design studio catering for the needs of the drinks, spirits and artisan food industries. From bespoke liquors, whiskeys, and artisan gins to craft beers, Backbar Studios' attention to detail and desire to create distinctive brand solutions has allowed them to grow as a studio along with their clients' diverse brands.

www.backbarstudios.com

P196–197

## Blurbstudio

Blurb is a design studio oriented to creating and implementing intricate branding strategies. They help to define new brands, reshape and develop those that already exist; they facilitate brands in reaching their target audiences and support them to maintain a positive public image. Blurb thinks and works in a multitude of disciplines. They believe that a well-designed brand exists not only as a series of pleasant images. A successful brand also creates meaningful experiences and strong bonds with its recipients.

www.blurbstudio.com

P198

## Carolina Akel

Carolina Akel is a freelance graphic designer and art director based in Chile.

www.behance.net/calala

P222

## Connie Huang

Connie Huang is a graphic designer. She graduated from Ming Chuan University with a degree in Communications Design. She excels at illustration and book design. She has published three poetry books.

www.behance.net/connie_huang

P200

## Fernando Díaz

Fernando Díaz is a graphic and type designer born in Montevideo, Uruguay in 1988. He is the co-director at TipoType Foundry and a teacher at ORT University.

www.fdiaz.org

P223

## Foxtrot Studio

Foxtrot is a graphic design studio from Warsaw. They are small, independent, and proud of it. With more than ten years' experience, they work with brands of all sizes from around the world. They strive to move the hearts and minds by joyful, honest and passionate design. Foxtrot loves to design visual identities, packaging and unique prints.

www.foxtrot.studio

P216

## Hio Cheng Choi

Hio Cheng is a graphic designer from Macau and based in Taipei. She has worked on a wide range of projects. In 2018, she established Hillz design. The studio is currently in charge of brand identity, packaging, web, UI, print for publications and exhibition design.

www.hillzdesign.com

P174–175

## Hsin-Yi Michelle Huang

Hsin-Yi Michelle Huang is a Christchurch-based graphic designer pursuing her passion for typography, brand design and packaging design. She is particularly interested in craft and the exploration into the field where East Asian typography encounters Western design.

www.hsinyih.co

P230–231

## Jens Nilsson

Jens Nilsson is a Stockholm-based, award-winning graphic designer, art director, branding expert and typographer with over 10 years' industry experience. He is the former art director at the Snask design agency and a 2004 Hyper Island alumnus.

www.jens-nilsson.com

P193

## Liao Wei

Liao Wei is a graphic designer and art director. He is the owner of L/g/s Studio. He also serves as a judge at design competitions and teaches design at the university level. He specialises in visual identity, book design and branding.

www.liaoweigraphic.com

P225

## Mauricio Arreola

Guadalajara-based graphic designer, Mauricio Arreola is the co-founder and creative director at Desierta.Studio. He is experienced in advertising, digital media, letters, illustration and branding. He always builds visual strategies from concepts and stories.

www.behance.net/Mauricio-Arreola

P210, 212

## MAYK Studio

MAYK is an Auckland-based, independent creative studio formed by Becky Ollivier. With capabilities across brand identity, packaging, illustration and visual communications, MAYK delivers idealed solutions that communicate distinctive and effective outcomes, helping brands evolve and connect with their people.

www.mayk.nz

P206, 217

## Mr Cup

Fabien Barral is a graphic designer whose innovative and unique designs attract clients from around the world. He is passionate about type and printing. He creates products like letterpress calendars, playing cards, magazines and posters. He sells and funds them on Kickstarter. He collaborates with clients to give life to their brands and projects and shares inspiration on the Internet. After years working under his own name, he now develops his own products under the Mr Cup pseudonym.

www.mr-cup.com

P178–179, 187

## Onion Design Associates

Onion Design Associates, a multi-disciplinary design studio based in Taipei, won in the Best Music Packaging category at both the 30th Golden Melody Award and the 44th Golden Tripod Award. Onion Design Associates was also nominated for Best Album Packaging at the 57th and 62nd Grammy Awards.

www.oniondesign.com.tw

P218–221

## Oscar Maia

Oscar Maia is a communication designer and art director based in the city of Porto, Portugal. Since 2008, he's been actively working on great projects alongside wonderful and talented people. Until 2014 he was part of Atelier Martino&Jaña's core team. From there up to 2017, he collaborated as senior designer with the multidisciplinary award-winning White Studio. Specialised in developing creative strategies applied in print, editorial, branding and web design projects, he presently works on a freelance basis with a wide range of clients dedicated to cultural industry and commerce. His work is recognised as being esthetically simple and bold, with a steady balance between great attention to detail, typography and composition.

www.oscarmaia.com

P226–227

## Sion Hsu

Sion Hsu studied visual communication and worked as a designer starting in 2011. He mostly designs for personal projects. He is also a curator. His works can be seen in magazines around the world, such as USA, Germany, France, UK, Spain, Iran, Malaysia, China, Japan, etc.

www.sionhsu.com

P199

## Steppe Magpie

Steppe Magpie makes beautiful embossed cards and invitations. The team loves minimalism, simplicity and creative experiments. They appreciate not only the appearance but also the content.

magpie.pro

P184–185

## Studio Bruch

Studio Bruch is a graphic design studio from Austria. Form follows idea. Bruch creates strong and distinctive visuals and strives for finding that certain something in any of their projects.

www.studiobruch.com

P172–173, 192, 194–195

## StudioPros

StudioPros designs with user experience and strategy. It is an award-winning studio driven by quality, detail and passion. They help clients to communicate their story and grow their brand with contemporary, thoughtful graphic design. Their client list includes international, national and regional companies, such as Facebook, IBM, Shutterstock and Lipton.

www.studiopros.work

P176–177

## Susu Studio

Under the loose umbrella of "creative direction", Susu works across a diverse range of creative fields with an even more varied list of projects. They pride on a socially-responsible approach to communicating with clever design. Rather than putting an emphasis on a particular style, the studio focuses on divergent research, long-lasting bonds with collaborators, and detailed, immersive solutions. This output has led them to flexibly work across projects from grassroots not-for-profits to multi-national tech companies.

www.susustudio.com

P229, 232

## The Counter Press

The Counter Press is a letterpress workshop and private press based in the UK. Combining modern thinking with traditional craftsmanship, they use wood and metal type printed at a wonderfully sedate pace, by hand, to create meticulously crafted typographic designs and limited edition print work.

www.thecounterpress.co.uk

P202–203

## vegrande®

vegrande® is a design studio focused on branding. It is established in Mérida, Yucatán, México since 2012. Their work involves strategy, conceptualization, visual and verbal identity, art direction, editorial, illustration, packaging and web design. Designers don't consider themselves having a defined style or working under a specific design current. They believe each brand should be unique. vegrande® works together with the mutual goal of making successful brands. It looks for innovative solutions using creative and critical thinking, artistic vision and various conceptual processes. vegrande® believes in design and aims to connect people and brands.

www.vegrande.mx

P228

## Victor Weiss Studio

At Victor Weiss Studio, designers are passionate about the process of creating visual brands. Being determined to make every project they undertake intelligent, functional and efficient for companies and people that look to stand out in the market. They incorporate history, values, mission statements and icons to create sophisticated, clean, modern designs that best represent the company's concepts. By picking their clients, the studio guarantees developing high quality sophisticated experiences.

www.victorweiss.com.br

P188–189

## We Are Büro Büro

We Are Büro Büro is an art, illustration and design collective based in Hamburg and Braunschweig, and is led by Julian Faudt and Stefan Mückner. Based on their shared roots in the fields of illustration, graphic design and graffiti, their passion flows into everything they produce: from branding, album covers, and illustrations to murals. The artwork of We Are Büro Büro opens a door to alternative realities in which clear forms, balanced colour palettes and playful, comic-like elements come together.

www.wearebuerobuero.de

P204–205

## xonxon

xonxon is a studio focused on interesting things. It is fascinated by the interactions between the world and all languages. Language is like the movies, literature or art. Each of them has affected people in different ways.

www.behance.net/chenshane

P211, 213

## Yao Yu Sun

Yao Yu Sun is a letterpress educator at Typesettingsg. Typesettingsg is a traditional letterpress studio focused mainly on handset types for printing. The studio conducts various types of letterpress workshops, letterpress design talks and print design using physical metal and wood types.

www.typesettingsg.com

P208–209

## Yu-Chen

Yu-Chen is a graphic designer who graduated from Chaoyang University of Technology in 2020. He is engaged in graphic design and motion design.

www.behance.net/u188499645

P201

## ジュディー DESIGN

Judith Cotelle is a French graphic designer who has lived in Hiroshima since 2007 and specialises in visual identity, packaging and editorial design. She likes to use patterns and imitate traditional craft techniques. She is the founder of ジュディー DESIGN.

www.judi-design.jp

P224

# ACKNOWLEDGEMENTS

We would like to express our gratitude to all of the designers and agencies for their generous contribution of images, ideas and concepts. We are also very grateful to many other people whose names do not appear in the credits, but who have made specific contributions and provided support. Without them, the successful compilation of this book would not have been possible. Special thanks to all of the contributors for sharing their innovation and creativity with all of our readers around the world.